D0898115

Devotion
to a
Calling

Devotion
to a
Calling

*Far-East Flying and Survival with
62 Squadron RAF*

GROUP CAPTAIN HARLEY BOXALL
& JOE BAMFORD

Pen & Sword
AVIATION

First published in Great Britain in 2010 by
Pen & Sword Aviation
an imprint of
Pen & Sword Books Ltd
47 Church Street
Barnsley
South Yorkshire
S70 2AS
Copyright © Group Captain C.H. Boxall & Joe Bamford
ISBN 9781848841499

Printed and bound in England by the MPG Books Group

Pen & Sword Books Ltd incorporates the imprints of Pen & Sword Aviation,
Pen & Sword maritime, Pen & Sword Military, Wharncliffe Local History,
Pen & Sword Select, Pen & Sword Military Classics and Leo Cooper.

For a complete list of Pen & Sword titles please contact
PEN & SWORD BOOKS LIMITED
47 Church Street, Barnsley, South Yorkshire, S70 2AS, England
E-mail: enquiries@pen-and-sword.co.uk
Website: www.pen-and-sword.co.uk

Contents

Acknowledgements

This book has only been made possible because of the help and cooperation of Group Captain Boxall's daughter, Sallie Hammond. She is also the goddaughter of Squadron Leader Arthur Scarf VC. and for many years the two men were close friends. Sallie has provided all the family photographs and her father's personal documents, to fulfil her burning ambition to tell his fascinating story.

The project has its origins in a meeting between Sallie, Arthur Lane and myself in Stockport during 2004, after they had made contact via the Internet. Eighty-eight year old Arthur is a Manchester Regiment veteran who joined up in 1935 and was later posted to Singapore. During his time as a POW he regularly witnessed cruelty and torture being inflicted on those who were unable to defend themselves.

Arthur was particularly angered when he discovered that after the British Army surrender in February 1942, hundreds of women had been murdered. Many of them were nurses and members of the Queen Alexandra's Nursing Service, as was Sallie's mother Pat, who fortunately escaped the carnage that was Singapore. Arthur has always been interested in all aspects of the war in the Far East and he was keen that the account of events written by Sallie's father should be published. As Arthur knew that my area of 'expertise' is the Royal Air Force he contacted me and introduced me to Sallie.

I would also like to thank Stan Fielding, Tim Tilbrook and Norman Hurst. Stan was an aircraft fitter on 62 Squadron and he served with both Group Captain Boxall and Squadron Leader Scarf. Stan gave valuable information about the evacuation of Singapore, Sumatra and Java, supplying details of terrible events that had been lodged in his mind since 1942.

Tim Tillbrook provided both motivation and valuable technical support, without which the book would probably never have been completed. Norman Hurst has been a source of knowledge on numerous occasions and provided me with copies of records and references. It has been very rare that Norman has not been able to supply the answer to one of my queries and without his help this account would have been much shorter and less detailed.

Finally I would like to thank my long suffering partner Janice, who spent many lonely evenings while I searched through files or tapped away at the keyboard. After meeting Sallie Hammond, Janice realized the importance of the project and she has been very supportive and understanding throughout.

Introduction

Devotion to a Calling is a unique story about a young man who joined the Royal Air Force in 1936 and who was serving in Malaya at the time of the Japanese invasion. He went on to lead the first operational sorties flown by the RAF in the Far East, flying ageing Bristol Blenheims that stood little chance against Japanese fighters that were superior in both numbers and technology. Subsequently he was lucky to escape from Singapore, Sumatra and Java, from where he had to swim out to sea and climb aboard a ship.

This is also a very special story because the first part was actually written by Group Captain Charles Harley Boxall himself, as he lay in hospital in India suffering from tuberculosis. Fortunately he survived his illness and lived for many more years but, because of the pressures of work and other commitments, he never found the time to complete his memoirs.

Group Captain Boxall's account gives a detailed description of flying training in the mid 1930s and the important events in his life, such as when he joined 62 Squadron just after it was formed in 1937 and when the unit re-equipped with the Bristol Blenheim and underwent its epic move from Britain to Singapore in August 1939.

In 1940 he ditched into the sea and, with the other two members of his crew, spent six days on a remote deserted island. He describes how they survived without food or water before being rescued by local fishermen.

Group Captain Boxall's manuscript forms Part One and it ends in September 1940. It is at that point that I continue his story in Part Two, to cover the devastating events in the Far East and the death of his close friend and colleague, Squadron Leader Arthur Scarf. From Malaya the story moves to India and recalls Group Captain Boxall's associations with the RAF airfields at Jodhpur and Mauripur, which he commanded between 1942 and 1944.

Finally there is mention of Group Captain Boxall's important role in 229 Group and his work with Transport Command, in building up its network of air routes and Staging Posts in India. He was a pioneer in the organization of trooping flights and he paved the way for the opening of air routes to the Far East, that were used by the RAF and civilian airlines such as BOAC and Qantas.

To give the book a more personal touch, Sallie decided that her father should be called Harley, rather being referred to in the text by his rank. That was the name everyone in the family called him and it was also the name by which he was best known to his friends and colleagues in the RAF

The hospital that Harley refers to at the beginning of his narrative in Part One is the Baragwanath Military Hospital near Johannesburg in South Africa. It was a sanatorium specifically run for the treatment and welfare of servicemen suffering from tuberculosis.

PART ONE

Prologue

It is nearly two years since I came to this hospital in South Africa, invalided from India. Two weary, unnatural years made more irksome as there is no pain from the disease from which I am suffering. I have lain on this bed so long, read so many books, written so many letters that I am at a loss to find something to occupy my mind, to keep me from thinking of the glory of the past and the obscurity of the future. And so, for want of something better to do, I am going to set down the story of the happiest days of my life; not that there is anything great or extraordinary about them, considering the times, but they wantonly portray some of the devotion and love that men can give to their calling.

Harley Boxall

CHAPTER 1

Elementary Flying Training

Charles Harley Boxall was born on 17 January 1913 in Handsworth, a district of Birmingham that had been incorporated into that city in 1911. Details of his life during his formative years are not known but from the age of eleven he was a student at King Edward VI Grammar School in Aston. The school was founded in 1883 but it had been rebuilt and reorganized in 1911. It was then made up of three separate sites with the main one, and the biggest by far with 250 pupils, being at Aston.

Girls had been admitted to the school in that year but strict discipline was in force and a twelve-foot high wall separated them from the boys; fraternization was not allowed. Harley transferred to the High School in 1927 that was part of the same establishment and his principal interests were noted as being swimming, tennis, rugby and horse riding. He became proficient in speaking French and German. He passed his matriculation examination in July 1929 and he left full-time education and went to work for the Accident and Guarantee Corporation as a clerk.

Harley was soon promoted and, in 1932, he passed the Insurance Institute's Examinations and was made an inspector. Despite that, for one so young and ambitious, it must have seemed a tedious job. In total contrast the RAF presented a challenge for any young man with a decent education and Harley was in many ways an ideal candidate.

For young men from the right background the RAF offered the

opportunity to embark on a career as an officer and potentially as a leader of men. Harley openly admits that he was seeking a more active way of life, but it is interesting to read that it was not the love of flying that attracted him to the RAF but a leaning towards a military life style. He had joined the Officer Training Corps at King Edward VI College in 1928, when his proficiency with a Colt revolver had been duly recognized.

When Harley joined the RAF in 1936 the service was undergoing expansion because of political tension in Europe. A rearmament programme had already been announced on 3 March by the Prime Minister, Stanley Baldwin. Up to that point the RAF comprised only sixteen fighter and twenty-four bomber squadrons, with another ten in secondary roles such as army cooperation duties.

Over the next few years many other squadrons would be formed with fast new types of monoplanes such as the Spitfire and the Hurricane, for the age of the biplane was rapidly coming to an end. However in the forgotten outpost of the Far East some would remain in service for several more years.

Harley does not name the station where he begins his story, or the unit where he carried out his elementary flying training, but it was 11 Elementary Flight Training School at Yatesbury in Wiltshire. Although it was controlled by the RAF, the flying training programme was carried out by instructors from the Bristol Flying School, one of many civilian organizations that were involved in the Air Ministry's expansion project.

How well I remember that day, Sunday 10 May 1936, when I set out on the greatest adventure of my life. I was a young man, twenty-three years of age, fit in mind and limb, and I had recently been granted a short service commission in the Royal Air Force. After an interview and medical examination at the Air Ministry some months before, I was about to report to the Elementary Flying School to which I had been posted.

My father had driven me down from my home in the Midlands and, within a few yards from the gates we had said goodbye, with some misgiving on my father's part as I know he was not at all sure that I was wise in giving up a secure job in an insurance office for a precarious and maybe hazardous four years in the RAF. But during the six years I had been in business life since leaving school, I had always felt that I was out place and that I could do better in some more active way of living.

Consequently when, at the end of 1935, the Air Ministry announced its scheme of Short Service Commissions, with the possibility of gaining a Permanent Commission, I grasped the opportunity as a means of escape from my everyday existence and sent in my application. I must confess that, unlike a lot of boys, I had never been mad on flying but since my days in the Officer Training Corps at school, I had always had a leaning towards a military life and that training was to stand me in good stead in my RAF career.

I watched the car disappear down the road and turned into the gates of the deserted camp, which was to be my home for the next two months. I must have been one of the first pupils to arrive for there was not a soul in sight. Carrying my suitcase I walked down an unmade pathway towards a large building which proved to be the administrative block. I reported at the commandant's office and soon afterwards I was shown to my room by a man who was to be my batman during my stay.

This flying school, at which my term was to be the first to be trained under the new RAF expansion scheme, was situated in the rolling downs of Wiltshire. Apart from an old hangar and one or two small buildings, all the accommodation was of recent construction; in fact it had only recently been completed for the commencement of the course. The lecture rooms and administrative block overlooked the grass airfield with the Mess and sleeping quarters behind it.

There were three blocks of sleeping quarters with about ten rooms in each. My room was on the first floor, well furnished with a bed, wardrobe, table, two chairs and a carpet and, above all, hot and cold water laid on. It would have done credit to a first class hotel. I unpacked my bags and made my way down to the Mess, anxious to see what else these new surroundings had to offer. As I entered the anteroom I saw that half a dozen other fellows had arrived and, introducing ourselves, we sat down to tea. Drawn together as we were, we were soon discussing our future life, the jobs we had left behind in Civvy Street, the way we got through the Air Ministry interview and the stiff medical board and, of course, aeroplanes.

As the evening passed, helped along with several tankards of beer, we began to feel quite at home in our new surroundings but this was not a party night. To nearly all of us this meant the beginning of a new career at which we had to make good. We had burned our bridges and the success of the future depended entirely on our own individual efforts. Looking back on that first evening I can see with what high hopes we regarded our new, unknown future. It was to be an adventure, a high privilege to wear the King's uniform and to most, like myself, an escape from the hum drum of commercial life. It proved to be a life in which one really lived, giving a sense of freedom which only those who have piloted an aircraft can hope to appreciate.

We retired to bed that night thinking that we were the luckiest fellows in England. It is sad to relate that several were returned to civilian life during the weeding out process of the next few weeks, and all but a few were to give their lives in the war three and a half years later.

The following morning at 0715 I was called by my batman with a nice cup of tea. Breakfast at 0800 and, at 0900, all the pupils assembled in one of the lecture rooms. There were twenty-four of us altogether, comprising eighteen pupil pilots (to be commissioned) and six leading aircraftmen (to become sergeant pilots). We rose to our feet as the commandant came into the room. A Scot who quickly put us at our ease, he gave us a general idea of the running of the school and the syllabus of our training. In two months we had to learn to fly and complete 50 hours of flying; in addition, to learn the theory of flight, how to navigate an aircraft, the rules of the air, the technical side of engines and airframes, the mechanics of bombing and gunnery and the administration of the RAF. In other words we were going to be very busy during the next eight or nine weeks.

The commandant finished his address by informing us that during this initial training period we would be under constant observation as to our suitability for entering the RAF as pilots and officers and that, unless we made the grade in both flying and in our studies, we should be returned to civilian life. I should mention that at this time we were still civilians, on probation, and that (in the case of pupil pilots) we should not be accepted and commissioned in the RAF unless we successfully completed this initial training.

When the commandant left, the chief flying instructor took over. He divided us equally into 'A' and 'B' Flights with the intention that while 'A' Flight was flying, 'B' Flight would be at lectures and vice versa alternate mornings and afternoons. He told us that the list of flying instructors and their respective pupils would be put up on the notice board and after a few words of advice and a kindly warning, he left us to go to stores and draw our log books, publications and flying kit.

It was quite a thrill getting equipped with a Sidcot suit, gloves, helmet, goggles and a parachute and, in spite of the strange hampered feeling in this rig-out, I began to feel I was on the way to becoming an aviator. Having put away all this equipment in our lockers in the crew room, we made for the notice board to see who our flying instructors were to be. The flying programme was also on the notice board and I saw that 'A' Flight, my flight, was due to fly the following afternoon, with lectures during the morning.

Up to now we had not seen much of the flying instructors as they all lived out of the Mess, but this morning they were much in evidence collecting all their pupils together and, no doubt, sizing them up. They were all very much of a type, nearly all having completed short service commissions in the RAF. To our eyes, of course, they were like Gods who were condescending to teach us mortals to fly. To their eyes, no doubt, we were just another batch of young men with whom they were destined to spend many weary hours trying to teach the young fools how not to break their necks.

My instructor fulfilled exactly my conception of a RAF pilot; weather tanned face with a bristling moustache and resplendent in white flying suit, white helmet and suede shoes. He used to roll up to the airfield in a large four-and-a-half litre Bentley Tourer with a black and white spaniel at his side. Notwithstanding this glamorous exterior, he was a very pleasant personality and an excellent instructor, and I owe him a debt of gratitude for his perseverance in helping me through the first major test of my flying career.

During the morning, all the aircraft had been brought out of the hangar and we had our first view of the machines with which we were to ride the skies. They were D.H. Tiger Moths, small biplanes with two seats, the instructor sitting in the front with the pupil in the rear cockpit. Wearing full flying kit, there was very little space to spare for even my medium build. They were all painted yellow, the colour for training aircraft, as a warning to pilots in the air to give a wide berth to this dangerous little craft in the hands of an incompetent beginner. We inspected them, we admired them, we sat in them and wondered whether we should ever take them into the air on a glorious first solo flight.

The following morning we got down to work in earnest. 'B' Flight were flying and we spent the morning at lectures, although it was difficult to concentrate with the noise of the engines being run-up on the tarmac and the thought of the 'B' Flight boys being first in the air. However ground studies were an essential part of the course and it behove us to settle down.

The morning passed quickly and after lunch I hastily donned my flying kit in preparation for my first instructional flight. Actually this was not my first experience of flying as, many years ago when I was a small boy at school, I had had a short trip in one of Sir Alan Cobham's aircraft which was touring England. But that was in a small airliner which did not create a lasting impression, not half so thrilling as wearing helmet and goggles with one's head out of the cockpit. Before long, my instructor came along the tarmac and signalled me to one of the Tiger Moths. Buckling on my parachute, I hobbled towards the aircraft. I climbed into the rear cockpit and was shown how to fasten the safety harness, two webbing straps over the thigh and two over the shoulders, all held together by a quick release pin – quick release in case one had to abandon the aircraft in a hurry and make a parachute descent.

Seeing me safely aboard, my instructor climbed into the front cockpit, fastened his harness and connected up the speaking tube. A voice came through the earphones:

'Can you hear me?'

'Yes sir,' I replied.

'This afternoon,' he continued, 'we are going to practise taxiing, and then I will take you into the air for some air experience.'

He called to the mechanic, who was standing-by to start up, at the same time explaining to me the procedure. First my instructor turned the switches off and the mechanic turned the propeller a few times to draw the petrol mixture into the cylinders. The mechanic then shouted 'contact' and my instructor, putting the ignition switches on, replied 'contact'. The mechanic then gave the propeller a hearty swing and the engine burst into life. With sufficient throttle to maintain a fast tick-over to warm up the engine, I was instructed in the procedure for testing the engine before flight. My instructor slowly opened up the throttle until the engine revolution counter was showing 1,800 rpm and tested the magneto switches to ensure that both magnetos were functioning properly and to see that the oil pressure was correct. Chocks in front of the landing wheels prevented the machine from moving forward but it was thrilling to feel the whip of the slipstream and the aircraft straining at the leash.

As a final test, the instructor moved the throttle wide open to see that the engine was giving the maximum possible revs and then slowly closed the throttle. It seemed strangely quiet after the roaring and tearing of the past half minute. On the signal 'chocks away,' given by my instructor waving his arms across his head, the mechanic pulled each chock from the wheels and the aircraft rolled slowly forward. The Tiger Moth is not fitted with brakes, so that the movement of the aircraft on the ground is controlled solely by the throttle and rudder, and by the ailerons to a limited extent, all of which helps to teach good airmanship.

With my feet on the rudder bar, my right hand on the control column (commonly called the stick) and my left hand on the throttle lever, I followed the movements my instructor was making on the dual controls fitted in his cockpit. We taxied along the edge of the airfield and soon my instructor told me to take over to see how I could cope. I gingerly opened the throttle, then a little more to get moving, turning the aircraft as instructed this way and that. Once I got used to the sluggish reaction of the aircraft to the controls, it was not too difficult. After a short time floundering around the airfield, the voice came through the earphones, 'I've got her now. Now we'll take-off and do some flying! Keep your hands and feet lightly on the controls and follow my movements.'

Keeping up his instructional patter, he taxied to the leeward side of the airfield and, after a careful look round for any other aircraft in the vicinity, turned into wind. Slowly he opened the throttle and the aircraft gathered speed. With the engine at full bore and tail up I felt a slight easing back of the stick and the aircraft was running lightly on its wheels, gathering speed every second. Very soon the wheels were off the ground and we were airborne.

It was difficult to concentrate on the flow of language coming through the earphones, as my instructor described each of his actions, in the thrill of this first flight in an open cockpit machine. The aircraft gently vibrated to the beat of the engine and the slipstream tore past my head. We climbed away from the airfield and levelled off at 2,000 feet. My instructor then proceeded to demonstrate the functions of the various controls; how the stick controls the upward and downward movement of the aircraft, how the rudder makes the aircraft turn to the left or right, how the ailerons dip the wings and how the movement of all three controls have to be coordinated to make a perfect change of directions. Soon it was my turn to try and, as instructed, I did my best to keep the machine 'straight and level'. For the first time in my life I was actually flying an aircraft! It was a strange, exciting new element to be in, to feel the power of the engine and the way in which the aircraft in the air responded to the slightest movement of the controls. I was rather surprised to see how slowly we appeared to be travelling over the earth's surface although the airspeed indicator showed 80 mph.

After about 30 minutes it was time to return. My instructor took over the controls and, making a beautifully banked turn, we headed back to the airfield. With the patter in my ears, I felt the movement of the controls as my instructor circled the airfield to the leeward side, easing back the throttle to lose height. Heading directly into wind, he closed the throttle and we glided down. Over the boundary hedge I could feel the stick coming back and back until, with the stick in the pit of my stomach, we touched down to a perfect landing. It was the end of a perfect day.

The days passed quickly in our new environment. Several of us used to go for a run round the airfield before breakfast and, with a game of tennis after tea, we kept very fit. During working hours lectures and flying instruction kept us fully occupied and most evenings we spent in private study. From the very beginning, my ultimate goal was a permanent commission and all my efforts were directed to this end.

Throughout my training I found the ground subjects interesting. Most of them were entirely new to me except for some technical knowledge of engines. As far back as I can remember I was always keen on motor cars and I found it relatively easy to assimilate the principles of the aircraft engine and its ancillary equipment. My small arms training in my school OTC also proved most useful. Theory of flight, navigation and airmanship were absorbing subjects, all essential and complementary to the actual piloting of an aircraft. The study of bombing, air gunnery and aerial photography brought home to us the militant side of our future profession. We explored the RAF Manual of Administration and King's Regulations and saw what a wealth of information there was in these two books by which the RAF was administered. This particular study was to prove invaluable in later days of my career as, in addition to flying duties, I was destined throughout the whole of my service to hold administrative jobs in one form or another.

We spent several hours a day in the air, weather permitting. With our instructors we learned to take-off, manoeuvre the aircraft in the air and land. We were quickly taught how to induce and recover from a spin; but aerobatics were left till later in the course. Our immediate aim was to go solo, and there was a lot of rivalry amongst us.

At last on 25 May, after doing a circuit and landing with my instructor, we taxied back to the leeward side of the field and he climbed out of the aircraft saying, 'She's all yours. Off you go.' The big moment had arrived. I think the excitement counterbalanced any trepidation that I felt. I opened the throttle and, within a few seconds, I was skimming the ground. Without the weight of the instructor, the aircraft was much lighter and without his head in front of me, I got much better forward vision. It was a thrilling experience being in the aircraft alone; a strange stimulating detachment from the earth. I gazed around my domain with an ethereal sense of freedom

Knowing my instructor was watching me from the ground, I carefully made an orthodox circuit of the airfield and prepared to land. It was easy enough to take the aircraft into the air, the most difficult part was to land in one piece. It had not been too difficult with my instructor in front of me, ready to grab the stick in case of emergency, but now I was on my own and I had some misgivings. However I had to come down to earth and, with my senses keyed, I turned into wind to make my first landing. Judging my approach, I eased back the throttle right up, re-set the trimming tab and with a quick glance at the air speed indicator, glided down to earth. I was over the boundary fence with the ground rushing towards me. Back a little with the stick, keep her straight, pick up that wing…only a few feet from the ground now, back a bit more…back…back…right back and (Heaven be praised) we were on the ground to quite a respectable landing. I had made my first solo flight, after 8 hours 30 minutes dual instruction. My instructor was quite pleased and I lapped up his congratulations. The other two had also gone solo that day and we celebrated that evening in the appropriate manner.

At the end of May, we had three days' Whitsun leave which I spent at home. I had not seen my family since the commencement of my training so there was a lot to talk about and many details to add to the news given in my hurried letters. I was relieved to find that my father had become reconciled to my new vocation and, indeed, was proud of his son's progress. As time went on his enthusiasm knew no bounds, and his weekly letters to me always provided a source of encouragement even in the darkest days ahead.

I returned to the flying school refreshed from the few days' rest and eager to acquire more proficiency and knowledge. With only a month to go to the end of the course, we quickly got back into our stride. Lectures kept apace with flying and within a fortnight I made my first solo cross-country flight, a distance of 100 miles, to Southampton and back. Having more or less mastered the art of taking-off and landing, aerobatics formed the greater part of our dual instruction. Loops and stall turns were fairly simple, but slow rolls required a lot of practise to make perfect. We also practised 'blind flying; the pupil being under a hood and flying the aircraft solely on instruments. This is a little uncanny at first, as having no visual horizon, one loses all natural sense of balance, but with practice one learns to place complete confidence in the instruments and it becomes quite good fun.

We had a short break at the end of June, most of us going up to London to the Hendon Air Pageant. We were thrilled at the sight of so much larger and powerful service aircraft than our Tiger Moths, knowing full well that we should be flying them within a matter of weeks.

With only a few days to go to the end of the course, we settled down to intensive study in the evenings in preparation for the final examinations. The papers were not too bad and the results, which came through several weeks later, placed me 3rd on the list. We also underwent a final flying test with a service instructor from the Central Flying School in which I felt I had not done too badly; at all events my instructor was quite friendly afterwards, so apparently I had not let him down.

Harley's certificate of competence and pilot's licence was awarded on 11 June 1936. Certificate Number 9744, authorized C.H. Boxall to fly 'All Types', although it very clearly stated that the licence was not valid for flying public transport aircraft. However this was only his basic flying qualification and he would have to wait several more months and undergo more rigorous service flying training before he got his RAF Wings.

CHAPTER 2

Service Flight Training School

Our course at the Elementary Flying Training School was now virtually at an end, and we spent the last day handing in our flying kit, making up our logbooks, paying Mess bills and generally getting cleared. We packed our bags for a short weekend leave prior to reporting to RAF Depot, Uxbridge, for a fortnight's Disciplinary Course. In spite of inclement weather, we had managed to complete the proscribed 50 hours' flying, of which half had been solo. We had received our 'A' licences from the Air Ministry, which licensed us to fly 'all types of private flying machines' and we were very proud of these small blue books which were material evidence of our flying ability. And to us pupil pilots this meant that we had successfully accomplished the first stages of our flying training and that we should now be gazetted as commissioned officers in the Royal Air Force.

During the two months I had been at this flying school it had truly become a second home to me, and it was with genuine regret that I said goodbye to my instructor and other members of staff. But the road lay ahead and I looked forward to the time when my training would be completed and I should be posted to a squadron as a fully qualified service pilot.

On 6 July Acting Pilot Officer Boxall was posted to RAF Uxbridge but he does not mention much about the time that he spent there. In his book *The Mint* T.E. Lawrence recalled his experiences at Uxbridge, which was then commonly referred to as the 'Depot'. In 1922 the training programme was based upon a strict regime that regularly involved humiliating recruits and forcing them to carry out the most menial tasks.

At that time Uxbridge was commanded by a one-legged officer who, Lawrence claimed, was something of a tyrant. By 1936 the tyrant had almost certainly retired but, as Harley himself notes, the tradition of treating recruits, and especially acting pilot officers, as the lowest form of life, remained in place.

I reported to the RAF Depot Uxbridge on Monday morning. It was like a self-contained town with hundreds of recruits still in civilian clothing and a good smattering of RAF uniforms. I soon made contact with my friends from my EFTS. Altogether there were about 100 of us ex-pupil pilots who had just graduated from Elementary Flying School. We were now acting pilot officers on probation, 'under suspicion'.

At 1000 we assembled in a large lecture room for an address by the camp commandant, a very military gentleman from whom we quickly learned that APOs comprised the lowest form of animal life in the Royal Air Force, and that during our two weeks at Uxbridge he and his staff were going to do their best to transform us into something resembling officers and gentlemen. After the comparatively unfettered life of the flying school, this was going to be discipline in earnest. We were visibly impressed by the commandant's speech, and heaved a sigh of relief when he departed.

That afternoon we were packed off to the city to make arrangements for our uniforms. There were several recommended military tailors and I went along to Gleaves in company with several of my friends. It was great fun being measured for service dress, greatcoat and mess kit, and all the other odd and ends, especially as we were not paying out of our own pockets. We were allowed by the Air Ministry an outfit allowance of £50 each, which just about covered the cost of the essentials.

The following morning we lined up on the parade ground for our first parade. We were a motley collection of all shapes and sizes, each in his own individual attire. Most of us wore sports coats and flannels, but some of the 'colonial troops' had some very natty suits. We all had to wear some headgear, and any passing observer might have gained the impression that this was a fashion parade. There was the ordinary trilby with the brim turned down, others with braided brim turned up; check golf caps pulled over the ears; Canadians with semi-cowboy hats; 'Anthony Edens' hobnobbing in green porkpies with a bristle up the side – in fact, all types were well represented except for the bowler. This, no doubt was out of favour as the bowler hat has a special significance in military parlance.

We were drawn up in two ranks and, after several attempts at numbering off, the fun really started when we tried to form fours. To a few, like myself, who had done this hundreds of times in our school OTC this was child's play but en masse it was a very ragged display which brought down the wrath of the flight sergeant drill instructor. Although he always addressed us as 'Gentlemen', it was obvious that he was calling us other names under his breath. However, as the days passed, we improved and by the end of the course we all had a fair idea what it was all about.

Apart from the drill, we had physical training every day and lectures on service life. We also had another fitting at our tailors in the city, and a final inspection of uniforms at Uxbridge by the camp commandant. During the course, we attended our first service dinner. Not yet having our uniforms, we wore dinner suits. Dinner was a parade and certain formalities had to be observed, such as when entering the anteroom, going up to the senior officer present and saying, 'Good evening, Sir.' When dinner was announced, we entered the dining room in order of precedence;

in other words we APOs brought up the rear. The meal was a solemn affair – the opposite to many which followed – and after the port had been passed and we had drunk the King's health, we were relieved when the senior officer rose and left the room, and dinner was at an end.

The last day we spent in packing, getting cleared from the depot, and some last minute shopping in the city. We had been informed to which RAF Flying Training Schools we were being posted, and half of us were going up to one in north Yorkshire. A lucky few were going straight out to the RAF FTS in Egypt. How we envied them. I think most of us at this early date, were anxious to serve overseas. On 18 June we left Uxbridge, without regret. It was another milestone passed, a little more experience gained. And now, ahead of us, lay the final stages of our training in which, all being well, we should gain our wings.

On 19 July Harley was posted to 9 Service Flight Training School at Thornaby, then in Yorkshire but now part of Teesside, situated four miles south of Middlesbrough. He informs us that at least half of his course from EFTS were posted to the station that housed 608 Squadron, a unit of the Auxiliary Air Force which was equipped with the Hawker Demon. At 9 SFTS Harley was to continue his flying training on the Hawker Hart, a variant of the light day-bomber that had first seen service in 1930.

We arrived at the RAF Flying Training School on Saturday afternoon and prepared to settle in for our six months' stay. Our first impression was that our standard of comfort was deteriorating as we progressed. This was entirely a wooden hutted camp, with temporary hangars constructed of wooden frames covered with fabric. Our quarters were of wood and fibre boarding, each with its own coal burning stove. During the winter these rooms were like ice boxes or furnaces, depending on whether the stove was off or on – there was no happy medium – but, as fires were not allowed until 1 October, this doubtful pleasure was held in store for us.

Hot and cold water was not laid on, instead we performed our minor ablutions out of wash basins and walked the length of a draughty passage for a bath. Of course none of this was real hardship, but one could not help compare the amenities with the comfort we had known at our civil flying school. Fortunately, the fellows of my EFTS were still together, so any disappointment we felt in our rude surroundings was quickly off-set by our high spirits and eagerness to get on with our training.

We soon learned that we comprised the junior term; the senior term, having already completed their first three months' training, were sporting their wings. It was very much like being at school again with the seniors looking down on the juniors, which example we followed when we became the senior term. There was no ill-feeling, just a healthy rivalry in games and on dinner nights.

The following Sunday, we were conducted round the station by one of the seniors performing the duties of orderly officer. Under his guidance, we acquired a good idea of the layout and pumped him dry with questions concerning the daily routine and the sequence of training. Among other things he told us that when the wind blew from a certain direction all the smoke from the neighbouring chimney stacks covered the airfield, completely obscuring the view of the ground from a few hundred feet up. He looked very gratified with our apparent dismay at this piece of information; we were still very young airmen, whose main concern was putting the aircraft safely back on the ground.

Next morning, we paraded for the first time in uniform. Our pride manifested itself in our bearing and smartness as we marched off to lectures. During the morning we were each summoned to an interview with the commanding officer, an elderly group captain complete with 'brass hat'. This was our first personal contact with a senior officer and we were somewhat relieved to find that, even after many years in the service, he had retained his humanity.

In the afternoon, we had our first view of the service aircraft we were to fly. Hawker Harts were to be used for dual instruction and, after going solo, we should do most of our flying in the Audax, which was a light bomber. The embryo fighter boys would also fly the Fury, and the Avro Tutor would be used for instrument flying practice. Altogether, there must have been some fifty aircraft lined up on the tarmac, all shining in their aluminium paint in the morning sun. To my mind, this Hawker series, with their two mainplanes, bracing wires and pointed nose, has always retained its beauty of design of design and air of pugnacity, even though long outmoded by the modern, streamlined monoplane with enclosed cockpit. Once having mastered the Hawkers with their powerful Rolls-Royce engines, and having used them in lethal practise with bombs and bullets, one acquired a new sense of flying and mastery in the air.

As at the civil flying school, we were divided onto two flights, with flying and ground subjects alternating mornings and afternoons. The flights were commanded by flight lieutenants and the instructors were flying officers and flight sergeant pilots, all with many hundreds of hours flying experience. Incidentally, a flight lieutenant in those days was regarded with greater respect and we had very little hope of attaining even this rank in our four years service.

It took me some little time to become attuned to the Hart after the Tiger Moth. The Hart was so much larger, more powerful and heavier. It required more skill in counteracting the torque produced by the 525 hp Kestrel engine which tended to swing the aircraft to one side. With engine throttled back, she glided at a much steeper angle because of her weight and landing required greater judgement as, in the last few seconds with the tail well down, the forward view was completely obscured by the engine cowling. There were many more instruments than in the Tiger Moth and, having a liquid cooled engine, the radiator, which wound in and out, required continual adjustment to maintain a temperature of 80 degrees centigrade.

For the first few weeks, we were constantly dogged by bad weather, high winds and low clouds, which curtailed flying considerably. It was almost a fortnight before I went solo in a Hart. This milestone behind me, practically all my training was done in an Audax. This is a Hart variant, a light bomber which used to be standard equipment in some RAF squadrons, the rear cockpit being fitted with a moveable Lewis gun for the air gunner.

The Hawker Audax was fitted with a 530 h.p. Rolls-Royce Kestrel engine and it had a top speed of 170 mph and a ceiling of 21,000 feet. The Audax, which could be distinguished from the Hart by the fact that it had a longer trailing exhaust pipe, had a maximum endurance of 3 hours and 30 minutes. It could be fitted with a synchronized Vickers machine gun in the forward position and a Lewis gun in the rear cockpit. Over 600 Audaxes were built, the last one being delivered in 1937, but over 200 of them were destroyed in flying training accidents before the war began.

Within a month, I successfully completed my first cross-country test, a triangular course of some 250 miles to Catfoss, onto Digby and back. Four days later on my second navigational exercise, I was not so successful. My course lay south to Grantham, a short leg to Nottingham and return. The weather at the start was not too good but as soon as I got south of the Humber it grew steadily worse and, to keep out of cloud, I was forced to fly at under 1,000 feet. The horizontal visibility was about a mile and before long I was completely lost – an unhappy position when one's time in the air is limited by the amount of petrol carried. After searching round for half an hour, I decided to head north for the Humber. Eventually it showed up and, pin-pointing my position on the map, I worked out another course to steer for Grantham and set it on my compass. This time I was more fortunate and I heaved a sigh of relief when the hangars eventually showed up through the haze. I landed feeling not too pleased with myself. This little flight had taken me 2 hours instead of 45 minutes! After refuelling I should have taken-off on the return trip straight away, but the visibility was such that the duty pilot at Grantham would not allow me to leave until three hours later, which was some comfort to my hurt vanity.

Altogether I now had 75 hours flying (including dual) to my credit and instruction was mainly concentrated on instrument flying and advanced aerobatics. For some time we had been endeavouring to fly at night but the weather had been so consistently bad that it had become almost routine for the programme to be abandoned after standing by for an hour or so after dark. These delays and postponements were not at all good for morale as the first flight into the night was thought about by most of us with a certain amount of apprehension. We were now accustomed to taking-off, flying and landing in daylight, but to do this in darkness was an unknown quantity which we were anxious, yet determined, to experience.

However, after nearly two months of the term had elapsed, my turn came. The weather had improved considerably except for a slight haze. The flare path had been laid out on the airfield and the engines were being warmed up. I climbed into the front cockpit of the Hart, with my instructor behind. On being given the green light by the duty pilot, we taxied out to the end of the flare path. Small cockpit lights dimly illuminated the instruments and, after a careful check, my instructor opened the throttle and took-off along a line of flares into the darkness ahead. It was a dark moonless night but as we gained height the street lights and illuminations of the neighbouring city came into view. I soon realized how pleasant night flying was. The air was smooth, there were no bumps such as one experienced in daylight, and civilization was below, with its twinkling lights.

We circled the airfield to come in to land. Aligning the aircraft with the flare path and judging our descent by the relative position of the flares, we came into a good landing. After one more instructional circuit, I went off solo. Once having breached the darkness, my pre-flight apprehensions disappeared and flying in solitude in the night I experienced a new stimulating detachment from the earth.

While I was cruising around, I saw another aircraft taking-off. I followed its navigation lights as it rose and left the flare path, when suddenly the lights went out. I looked again and within seconds, a sheet of flame spurted out of the ground. I was too concerned in bringing my aircraft in to land to give this much thought, but after landing, I learned that an APO, one of my close friends, had crashed soon after take-off. The flames I had seen had been his funeral pyre. His military funeral was the first that I attended but, unfortunately, it was by no means the last.

On the ground we continued our studies. We advanced further into the subject commenced at civil flying school and, in addition, we studied higher mathematics, meteorology and signals. When we arrived we had each been issued with a 'buzzer', a small keyboard fitted with a battery on which to learn the Morse code. We had to attain a proficiency of eight words a minute and any evening, down the corridor of our quarters, could be heard the high pitch buzz of our practising.

Apart from our lectures, we spent many hours on the parade ground with rifle and bayonet, drilling and being drilled. Here again, my school OTC training proved its worth. We also had to take turns performing the duties of orderly officer and duty pilot. The orderly officer's tour of duty was twenty-four hours. He was responsible for the supervision of the guard and the issue of rations, the barracks, attending the airmen's meals, investigating complaints and many other duties. At night he was responsible for the safety of all buildings, which necessitated at least one tour of the station after midnight. A long, but not very hardous day.

The duty pilot was also on for twenty-four hours. He was concerned with matters exclusively concerned with flying, and was responsible for aerodrome discipline and serviceability of airfield equipment. He logged the arrival and departure of all aircraft, kept all weather information and initiated action in regards to aircraft overdue or in distress; all very interesting and instructive.

The end of term examinations were looming and most of our evenings were spent in private study. It was of vital importance to do well in these exams as they directly affected our promotion to the rank of flying officer. Occasionally we would go into the neighbouring city, but there was nothing attractive about it and it had little to offer apart from two or three cinemas. In fact most of our life was spent on the station, with its full working days, sport on Wednesday afternoons and Dinner Nights twice a week. Soon we were ploughing through the written examinations. This was the culmination of our intensive ground studies as next term all our time would be spent in the air.

Then came the flying test with the chief flying instructor and, shortly afterwards, our names were posted as having qualified for the flying badge. At last we could wear the much coveted wings on our breast. Judging by the rapidity which these appeared on otherwise unadorned tunics all the APOs, including me, had furtively obtained a pair in readiness for this great occasion. Finally, the whole school paraded for inspection by the AOC, Training Command.

Harley was awarded his wings on 3 October 1936 but there was still some way to go before he passed out. Having completed the first half of the course he and the other successful students joined the Advanced Training Squadron. Up to this point the emphasis had been mainly on his flying skills but the advanced training in the second term concentrated on air reconnaissance, air gunnery and aerial bombing.

For the senior term, this was their passing out parade and shortly they would be posted to squadrons; for us, this meant we had successfully accomplished the first half of our service training. Another three months and we too would be joining a squadron. Feeling very proud of myself, I packed my bag and went home for three weeks' well earned leave.

I returned from leave with renewed vigour and enthusiasm. It was good to see my old friends again as they drifted in from all parts of the British Isles. We looked forward immensely to this term when practically all our time would be spent in the air, culminating in five weeks at an Armament Training Camp, and this term we were the senior term, and assumed the usual air of superiority over the pupils arriving from Elementary Flying Training School.

At the end of the previous term we had been given the opportunity of stating to which type of squadron we would like to be posted, but our individual flying ability and temperament influenced the final decision made by the chief flying instructor. We knew that those with nautical experience would go on flying boats, the devil-may-care boys would go to fighters, the steadier types would be posted to medium bombers and the remainder to light bombers. My first choice had been for flying boats but I was quite satisfied when I learned that I had been earmarked for medium bombers – my second choice – which meant, in all probability, flying the latest twin-engined machine, the Rothermere bomber, later to be called the Blenheim Mark 1.

The pilots designated for medium bombers were paired off, so that while one was flying the aircraft the other would be in the rear cockpit to practise navigation, aerial photography, bombing and air firing. A friend of mine, Dan, a Canadian, agreed to fly with me and I think I got the better half of the bargain as he had had quite a lot of flying experience in Canada before coming over to join the RAF. Such was his keenness that he had worked his passage across the Atlantic in a cattle boat and I am sure, judging by the way he used to sniff the air, he had never quite got the aroma out of his nostrils.

We were soon off into the air to get back into flying practice. First Dan flew the aircraft and I acted as the observer, standing in the rear cockpit enjoying the new experience of being a passenger. I was wearing the observer type harness, secured to the floor of the aircraft by a steel 'monkey chain' which clipped to the parachute harness between the legs. Our speaking tubes were connected so that we could converse. To try the bomb aiming position, I had to double myself up and slide head first beneath the pilot's seat, then open a panel in the floor to obtain an uninterrupted view of the ground beneath.

In bombing practice, we were to spend many hours in this position, breathing in hot oily fumes from the radiator in front. We cruised around for about an hour, did a few aerobatics and landed. Changing places I took Dan up in the back. After some time, I made some remark through the speaking tube and got no answer. I repeated it but still no reply. I twisted round to see what had happened. Dan was not in the rear cockpit. I suddenly remembered that a short time before we had gone through a particularly bad bump and I was stricken with panic at the thought that Dan had been jolted out of the aircraft. The observer's parachute pack is stowed away, to give him greater freedom of movement, and I knew that if my fears were justified he had plunged to certain death. I started to circle down in the hopeless quest of finding him when his helmeted head came up into the rear cockpit.

'Where the hell have you been,' I said, 'Didn't you hear me calling you?'

'No,' he replied nonchalantly, 'I was just having a look round below.'

What I said to him when we landed cannot be put into print.

It was not long before we got down to work in earnest. Flying every day, weather permitting, we practised finding wind speed and direction as preliminary to bombing. When we had produced satisfactory results at this, we were sent off on a simulated bombing over the camera obscura. In the air the method was identical to live bombing except that, instead of releasing a bomb, the observer exploded a magnesium bulb when the target was in his sights. This flash was seen on the ground and plotted on a chart. It was not until the aircrew had landed that they could see how near they had been to 'hitting' the target. To get good results, it required complete cooperation between the pilot and observer – the pilot to act quickly on the observer's corrections, at the same time maintaining a steady height and speed, and the observer to be accurate in his computations and sightings. Dan and I alternated as pilot and bomb aimer and our perseverance was later rewarded when we went to Armament Practice Camp and dropped real bombs.

Many hours were spent in camera gun practice. The gun was fitted in the rear cockpit on a moveable ring, in place of the Lewis gun, and instead of pouring bullets into the target, we took photographs of it. This was quite good fun as it meant some authorized low flying. We used to fly over to the range – actually a field in which a large white board was set up – and circle at about 200 feet shooting off several rolls of film. The results were assessed after the film had been developed.

About a fortnight after our return, Dan and I set out on a cross-country flight to Northolt, on the outskirts of London, a distance of 230 miles. We flew down in the morning and arrived in time for lunch. The weather had been pretty foul all the way but, unfortunately, it was not bad enough to prevent our return, otherwise we might have spent a pleasant weekend in London. It was Friday, the 13th of the month but despite a safe return to base, we decided that the Fates had not been very considerate.

A week later we had a more exciting time. It was the middle of November and we were somewhat late taking-off for a flight to Doncaster and back. All went well for the first half of the trip but about halfway back the wintry sun set and we eventually arrived over the airfield after dark. Rockets and Very lights were popping up all over the place but there was no flare path and I do not think Dan was too happy in the back. However, he strapped himself in, prepared for the worst, and I landed the aircraft in one piece. We proudly logged another 30 minutes night flying, and began to think that we were earning our 11s 10d per day.

As the winter set in, the weather steadily deteriorated. Days of continuous heavy rain transformed the airfield into a sea of mud which caused many minor accidents. In the boggy ground deep ruts were ploughed by the aircraft landing wheels and, to make things more difficult, the heavy frost which followed solidified the ruts. As though the elements were making quite certain that we should not leave the ground, we had a week of continuous fog. We filled in the time with drill and lectures.

At last the weather cleared and we started to learn formation flying. This required a lot of practice to perfect and was rather tiring at first, but with experience it became quite good fun. We polished up our night flying and I went off on a 2 hour 30 minute cross-country, getting to bed at 0600. Unfortunately we lost another of our APOs when he dived into the sea at night, leaving no trace.

It was at this time that we learned with sorrow of the abdication of King Edward VIII. When my commission came through some time later, it was one of the comparatively few which bore his signature. I regret that I no longer have it with me; it was lost with the rest of my belongings during the war in the Far East.

For some time I had been thinking of buying a car. We had not been allowed to keep them during our junior term but they were permitted to the seniors.

Eventually I completed negotiations and a hire purchase agreement with a local motor engineer who was a well known racing motorist. I had a certain amount of difficulty in persuading an insurance company to accept my proposal as they all seemed to think that a RAF pilot with a sports car was the world's worst risk. However, after agreeing to bear the first £5 of any claim I received my policy and found myself the proud owner of a 1932 Wolseley Special. It was a very sporting job, pale blue with very good performance. I hade a lot of fun with this for a few months until my dwindling bank balance made it necessary to dispose of it.

Harley was very enthusiastic about motor cars and motor sport and at one point he typed up a list of every vehicle that he had owned. He eventually traded in what he described as a Wolseley Hornet for a Morris Oxford, before exchanging that for an MG. He also owned a Ford 8 and Hillman Aero that he used when he was on leave in Birmingham.

After an enjoyable five days leave at home over Christmas 1936, I returned to an atmosphere of feverish activity as our period at the Armament Practice Camp had been brought forward and there was much preparation to be made prior to departure. We fitted guns and bombsights to our aircraft and re-swung compasses to take out any deviation caused by this added amount of metal. The sights of the front Vickers gun were aligned and the air speed indicators and altimeters calibrated to ensure accuracy in bombing.

We could not all travel by air to this camp, seventy miles away on the Yorkshire coast, so I elected to go by road in my Hornet, and a very enjoyable drive it was over the moors. The sun was shining and I cruised along at 50-60 mph for most part of the way. The last ten miles or so were along narrow winding lanes and I eventually arrived at this out-of-the-way station. The buildings were very similar to those at FTS, except that our quarters were larger – and consequently colder. The airfield, if anything, was in a worse state than the one we had left.

The morning after our arrival we went down to the range by road, some ten miles away, for instruction by the armament officer in bombing and range signals and to get a general idea of the layout. The targets for the air-to-ground firing were set up on the edge of the cliff and the bombing targets, floating platforms, were about half a mile out to sea. The next five weeks formed the climax of our service training, and we were all looking forward immensely to firing real bullets from our guns and dropping live, if only practice, bombs. The hours of training would be put to the test, and we were about to get our money's worth!

During our stay the weather persisted in its perversity. We had rain and snow, and the airfield got steadily worse. But we took advantage of every break in the elements, flying according to the programme from dawn till dusk. Dropping bombs was quite good fun, but the real sport was practising with the front gun. The gun is fixed and aligned with the aircraft, so the pilot had to sight the aircraft on to the target. In air-to-ground practice this meant swooping down from 1,000 feet, getting a burst of bullets into the target and pulling up a few feet from the sea; then up and round again for another go. Firing at the drogue – rather like a wind sock, towed by another aircraft – was the most exciting of all as this simulated air combat; rather one sided perhaps as the drogue could not fire back, but nevertheless thrilling to get in a burst of fire and pull away with inches to spare.

The days flashed past and soon it was time to return to FTS. Dan and I had good cause to be pleased with our efforts as, together, we had obtained the best bombing results of the course. He had put up the best score on the drogue and I had made a record score on the ground target.

Back at FTS, it was only a few days to the end of the term and we eagerly awaited our postings. I was delighted when I learned that I had been posted to a squadron in Berkshire – a squadron with a fine record in the 1914-1918 war – and was overjoyed at the thought of leaving the cold and drabness of the north. We proudly marched past at our passing out parade and celebrated too well at dinner that night.

This was the parting of the ways. We, who had started together at the civil flying school eight months before, were now setting out in twos and threes to a new life which would take us to all parts of the Empire. We had made firm friendships that would not be forgotten and many of us were to meet again in fleeting moments during our travels in the years that lay ahead.

Harley completed his course at SFTS on 20 February 1937 with an overall pass mark of 78 per cent. It was noted on his service record that he was a 'Good average pilot. Above average at Ground Work.' Those brief observations and particularly the comment about ground work would influence the way that his future career in the RAF would progress.

CHAPTER 3

62 Squadron

I drove down from FTS to my new station in Berkshire: first impressions were excellent. The Mess was like an old country house and had acquired all the comforts and amenities which go with an established station. I was shown to my room on the first floor, overlooking the gardens. It was well furnished, with hot and cold water laid on and a cheerful fire burning in the grate. I felt I was going to be very comfortable in my new home. The Mess was occupied by some fifty officers of two squadrons who, at first, were inclined to stay rather aloof from a fledgling from FTS but happily I was not alone as one of my contemporaries, a Scotsman, had arrived to join the same squadron. Mac and I walked round the station in the evenings and were impressed with its orderly layout and well constructed buildings. It exuded a friendly atmosphere, acquired from many years of habitation.

The following morning we reported to the station adjutant, then to our new CO in the squadron hangar. We received a friendly welcome and were allotted to flights, Mac going to 'A', whilst I went to 'B' Flight. Our squadron was equipped with Hawker Hinds, a machine similar to the Audax but with supercharged engines giving more power and speed.

Pilot Officer Boxall was posted to 40 Squadron that was stationed at Abingdon and equipped with the Hawker Hind. The Hind was of a similar design to the Audax that he had flown at 9 SFTS, but it was fitted with a more powerful 640 hp fully supercharged Rolls-Royce V engine. It had a maximum speed of 186 mph and it was armed with a Vickers gun forward and a Lewis gun in the aft position. It was capable of carrying a 500 lb bomb load.

After the pressure of training days, it was somewhat difficult to settle down to the comparative ease of squadron life, with its paucity of flying and ground duties. After an instructional flight in a Hind I went off solo and I found this aircraft very pleasant to fly, even more manoeuvrable than the Audax. I flew down to my old civil flying school, but did not land as it appeared to be deserted. It was strange to look again at the place of my earliest endeavours, with all its familiar landmarks; and it seemed ages since the day when I first reported there to take up flying; so much had been crammed into the past nine months.

A few days after our arrival, Mac and I were summoned to an interview with the AOC Bomber Group. He gave us a short address on the responsibilities of young officers and we came away with the impression that between us we were carrying the whole weight of the RAF on our shoulders.

I was just beginning to feel settled in the squadron when, within a month of my arrival, I was posted again. I heard with dismay that I was to join a new squadron forming in County Durham. With a heavy heart I packed my bags and drove the 250 miles back to the cold and dismal north. To add to my gloom I collected a summons for exceeding the speed limit through Leicester that later cost me £1 and an endorsement on my driving licence.

Harley had been with 40 Squadron for just over five weeks when he was posted to 103 Squadron on 1 April. On reflection he may have considered himself lucky. The following year it was re-equipped with the Fairey Battle and suffered heavy losses in France while part of the Advanced Air Striking Force in France.

I eventually arrived at the mess, stiff with cold at 2300 only to find that I was not expected and that I should not have been there, anyway. Apparently, somebody had slipped up on the posting and I should have reported to a station forty miles from whence I had come, where the new squadron was forming and receiving its Hinds prior to flying up to this benighted hole as soon as the airfield became serviceable. Tired and miserable, I found an empty room, made up a bed and passed out.

In the morning I discovered that were only three other officers on the station and that they were in the process of opening it up. It was of the same matchboard construction as the FTS I had left, only the surroundings were about ten times worse, right in the middle of slag heaps and chimney stacks. I reported to the CO and, having no job for me, he straight away packed me off on 14 days' leave. I headed south and drove home the 200 miles, secretly hoping that I should never see the place again.

Harley was describing RAF Usworth, a former First World War airfield that was destined to become a sectors station in 13 Group just after the war broke out. His observations about the environment were accurate and the airfield was later relegated to training duties because of the amount of industrial haze and pollution. There were only limited facilities at Usworth but the station later had strong associations with 607 Squadron of the Auxiliary Air Force. 103 Squadron was the first permanent unit to be posted to Usworth and it remained there until September 1938. Many years later the airfield was to become Sunderland's Municipal Airport.

I disposed of my Hornet while on leave and returned north by train, determined to make the best of things. But a very pleasant surprise awaited me. I had been detailed to attend a conversion course on to twin-engined high speed monoplanes and within a few hours I was on the train again to a station in Norfolk. On arrival, I found that I had just missed seeing my co-pilot, Dan, who had been on the previous course; but I recognized an old 1924 Delage Tourer in front of the mess and located its owner, my old friend Mac, who had also arrived for training. Our conversion was about to take place on Ansons, twin-engined but not very high speed cabin monoplanes. I was more than delighted at this turn of events, as I had been afraid that I had missed getting on to twin-engined aircraft. The course was to last for four weeks and in this period we had to qualify and complete 10 hours solo flying. The station, situated in pleasant country, was well founded and our short stay was most enjoyable.

On 1 April Harley was posted to Bircham Newton in Norfolk to train with 206 Squadron which was a general reconnaissance and training unit equipped with the Avro Anson. The course ran from 3 April to 1 May and so presumably his leave was not much more than a 48-hour pass. He passed the course with flying colours achieving a mark of 72 per cent.

I had 1 hour 30 minutes' dual with an experienced pilot and then went off solo. The Anson was a very pleasant aircraft to fly. Being a cabin machine one could dispense with helmet and goggles and, instead of the normal pilot-type parachute, one simply wore a parachute harness. In the air, the aircraft could be trimmed to fly itself, with hands and feet off the controls. Taking-off was comparatively easy as the twin-engines counteracted any inherent swing and landing was simple as long as the pilot judged his approach and touch down just inside the boundary fence; otherwise, as the aircraft tended to float, there was a consequent danger of overshooting. In spite of being incapacitated for a week with my annual dose of flu, I managed to complete my 10 hours solo within the period of the course.

I had only been back at my station in the north of England a matter of days when I was informed that I had been posted again, to a new squadron which was forming in Berkshire, in fact at the delightful station which I had left six weeks before. I was overjoyed at this piece of news and gladly packed my bags for the journey southwards, secretly praying that the Air Ministry would at last allow me to settle down in my new squadron.

As the narrative will show, my wish was granted and I helped to form and lived and worked with this squadron for the next five years; such happy memorable years. We started from nothing and built up a fighting formation which was second to none. Though later to be decimated in a far distant land, it fulfilled its destiny in defence of the Empire.

The squadron was originally formed in 1917 and equipped with Bristol

Fighters. After a conspicuous war record it disbanded in 1919. We, in 1937, were now going to re-form the squadron. Temporarily, our aircraft would be Hawker Hinds but later we should be equipped with Bristol Blenheims.

Full of enthusiasm, I reported to my new CO, a young flying officer who was filling the position pending the arrival of a squadron leader. The officers and airmen to form the squadron were arriving every day and, amongst the officers were four who had been in the senior term of my FTS. We were to become close friends and besides myself, Pongo, Bertie and Ken remained with the squadron for the best part of five years.

This was 62 Squadron at Abingdon where Harley was posted on 7 May. Its first CO was Squadron Leader Edward Frank Nutall. Pilot Officer Arthur 'Pongo' Scarf was one of the first officers posted in to the squadron and he and Harley had first met at 9 SFTS, where Pongo had been in the senior term with five months' seniority over Harley. After leaving Thornaby Pongo had been posted to 9 Squadron at Scampton where he had flown the Handley Page Heyford biplane bomber.

From there Pongo had been sent on a twin-engined conversion course similar that which Harley had experienced, but with 206 Squadron when it had been based at Manston in Kent. After completing his course Pongo was posted to 61 Squadron at Hemswell before being posted again, on 18 April, to 62 Squadron. Pilot Officers Keegan (Bertie) and Irving (Ken) were also friends from 9 SFTS and they were all destined to be posted out to the Far East with the unit.

Some might think that it was unusual for junior officers who were straight out of training to be appointed to duties such flight commander or adjutant, but this was as a result of Britain keeping such a small peacetime air force. By 1938 there was a shortage of experienced officers, in particular those holding the rank of flight lieutenant. Even though the time that it took to gain promotion from flying officer was cut from four years to two, on a lot of units it was still necessary for junior officers to be appointed to key positions.

One of the CO's first actions was to appoint his officers to the various squadron duties. Pongo and Ken became flight commanders, being the most senior of the APOs, and Bertie became signals officer. The CO asked for a volunteer to become squadron adjutant and, liking the sound of this title, I jumped at the opportunity little knowing how much was involved. The adjutant, as the confidential staff officer of the CO, is responsible for all routine matters within the unit which, if the unit is established, is a fairly simple matter. But, with the squadron in process of forming, with new personnel and equipment arriving daily, I soon found myself inundated with paper work.

It was all new and vastly interesting but, unfortunately, it considerably curtailed the time I was to spend in the air. At this time the squadron was intensively practising with other squadrons for a mass formation flight for the Hendon Air Pageant a few weeks hence. When the time came, I was disappointed at being unable to take an active part in the mass fly past but I was there as a spectator and, meeting a lot of my old training school pals, we spent a boisterous night in London.

At this time, in addition to forming the squadron, we had to make arrangements to move to another station in Buckinghamshire, which was to be our permanent base. Our new CO, an elderly squadron leader, had arrived to take over command of the squadron at the end of June and I flew over with him to inspect our new home. We were very impressed. This was a brand new station, well laid out and solidly built. It was due to be ready for occupation in about a month's time and, after making preliminary arrangements for taking over the domestic and technical accommodation for the squadron, we flew back home the odd thirty miles.

The squadron was preparing to move to Cranfield, eight miles south-west of Bedford, where it would share the airfield with 82 and 108 Squadrons. It is unclear as to whether the 'elderly CO' was Squadron Leader Nuttall, who was the CO when the squadron reformed, or Squadron Leader Johnson who took over from him, some time in June. At about the same time Pongo Scarf was promoted to flying officer and sent to Manston for a short navigation course. He later re-joined 62 Squadron at Cranfield and became part of 'A' Flight.

I began to feel the need for a car of my own again and, finances having improved somewhat, I bought a Morris Oxford Six coupe; a handsome motor car but with the unfortunate habit of melting big end bearings. However it provided transport for several happy weekends with my people sixty miles away, but it became apparent that an expensive overhaul was the only lasting remedy to this bearing trouble so I put it back on the market.

In July, the squadron moved to its new base in Buckinghamshire. Another squadron also moved in and it soon became apparent that it was going to be a very happy station. Our daily routine started at 0800 with the colour hoisting parade. Except on Saturday morning when the station commander took the salute, the squadron adjutants, their squadrons on the parade ground, inspected the ranks, marched past the saluting base and then to the hangars for the days' work. Officers and men went back to their flights and before long the roar of the engines running up on the tarmac announced the commencement of the flying programme. Some went off on cross-country flights, others on formation flying and, when the range was allotted to us, practice bombing at Otmoor.

Although I was finding more time for flying these days, my administrative duties kept me in my office most of the time. First thing in the morning, I would go through the correspondence with my CO and draft replies for his signature. New arrivals to the squadron had to be interviewed and allotted to quarters, and defaulters brought before the CO for judgement. Squadron orders had to be drawn up, and my signature must have appeared on thousands of leave passes. The innumerable returns required by the higher authority and the pressing need to bring this new squadron, still in its infancy, to a pitch of operational efficiency in the shortest possible time kept me extremely busy. It was an invaluable experience to me, to have such a responsible job so early in my service career, but it could have been made a lot easier had I had a less neurotic CO. As it was I think he put ten years on my life.

After working hours, our home was the Mess and a very happy place it was too. There were thirty young officers living-in, comprising the two squadrons, and we were all much of the same age, with the same zest for life. At that time, an officer was not allowed to marry until he had attained the age of thirty, or the rank of squadron leader, so we were all carefree bachelors living very comfortably, if all a bit short of money. However, somehow, most of us managed to run some sort of car, but the various mechanical objects parked outside the Mess were certainly not in keeping with the pretentious surroundings.

We were obliged to dine in the Mess three times a week and once a month we had a guest night when we wore Mess kit. Our guests must have thought that they had been invited to a mad house as these evenings usually devolved into a shambles when furniture was upended and the anteroom cleared for various games. Fortunately, seldom were bones broken, but the following morning produced many aches and pains not to mention a general hangover shared by all members. However, the air the following morning usually cleared the aching brow and, personally, I always found the oxygen mask a very good reviver.

On our free evenings, we usually migrated to the nearest town, some seven miles away. It was quite a pleasant county town with a couple of cinemas and several hotels, one of which we always looked upon as our headquarters. It was here that I met Maureen.

Up till now I had had no serious attachments to women; only a series of girlfriends in my home town but nothing deep enough to carry with me into my new life. When I first saw Maureen I knew we were destined to fall in love. Petite, with fair wavy hair and laughing blue eyes, we found so much in common and she filled the place in my life which I realized had been empty up to the moment of our meeting. Dear Maureen, when I think back to the two short years we had together, I realize how happy we were and I think you should have married me – I asked you several times but you were always afraid that any legal obligations to one another would depreciate our love. And being young, and happy in our love, we left it at that.

In November, the squadron moved to an armament training camp in Dorset for three weeks' intensive bombing and air firing practice. We were on the go from dawn till dusk, cramming in as many flying hours as the weather made possible. And when I was not in the air, I was in my office catching up on paperwork.

We had a very interesting interlude with the Navy during our stay at the coast. In company with several of my fellow officers, I went out in a submarine for the day. We spent most of the time under water while surface craft endeavoured to locate us with their Asdic and we had one anxious moment when, through the periscope, it was seen that a destroyer was bearing down on us. Only by going into a crash dive did we avert being rammed. This break in our normal routine, apart from its official purpose of liaison with another service, was most instructive and I think we all felt great admiration for these men trained to fight underwater. I know I felt glad to see the blue sky again.

I spent Christmas 1937 with my people at home and, returning to my station early in the New Year, found that we were being packed off again to the armament training camp for two weeks. But the weather at the coast was so consistently bad during our stay that we got in very little flying.

On our return, we were informed that we should be re-equipped with Blenheims in February. This was what we had been looking forward to for the past year as the Blenheim Mk I was the most up to date bomber to be introduced into the Royal Air Force and we were the second squadron to receive them. We had heard quite a lot about Blenheims, and several disturbing stories about how they blew up in the air for no apparent reason. There had been several obscure accidents, nevertheless in the four years that we flew them we found them very well behaved and completely free from any vice, a wonderful aircraft to fly but, as we found out later, with poor defensive armament.

After many years Harley's memory let him down as 62 Squadron was not the second unit to be equipped with the Blenheim but the fifth. The first to receive them was 114 Squadron in March 1937 when it was based at Wyton. Then 30, 44, 90 and 144 Squadrons were all re-equipped before 62 Squadron finally received its first Blenheim in February 1938.

It was very pleasant again flying in a cabin machine and the two mighty Hercules engines gave one a greater sense of security, especially when flying over the open sea. Up to that point with our Hinds, the crew had comprised a pilot and air gunner/bomb aimer. But the Blenheim's crew was three, a pilot, an observer who navigated and aimed the bombs, and an air gunner who was also the wireless operator. All this meant that our erstwhile air gunners had to undergo intensive training as wireless operators and we had an influx of air observers into the squadron.

This reorganization meant a lot more paper work for the adjutant and life was very full, and very pleasant. One of our officers, Taffy, a keen sailor, had bought a boat which he kept on the east coast. It was originally a fishing boat, a 40 ft ketch, and on many occasions four or five of us used to spend the weekend sailing in the North Sea. This boat had obviously seen better days and once, when the seas were particularly rough, we sprung a serious leak at the bowsprit which necessitated continually bailing for several hours before we made safe harbour.

'Taffy', was officially known as Pilot Officer, later Wing Commander, Frank Griffiths. He, like Pongo Scarf, was a keen sailor. Pongo had been so keen to go to sea that he had originally applied to join the Royal Navy but was judged to be unsuitable and turned down. The Navy's loss was the Air Force's gain and his skill as a pilot was soon recognized. The elements of wind, speed and drift are common to both sailing and flying although it sounds as if they were all better pilots than they were sailors.

To counteract the severity of the weather, we used to wear our old flying boots and all the old clothing we could find. Our appearance was thoroughly disreputable. I remember on one occasion after twenty-four hours in the North Sea we tied up at some small harbour on the east coast and went to explore the town. Late in the evening, we landed up at some working men's club where, for some unknown reason, we adopted a 'Scandinavian' accent in keeping with our filthy appearance. We were welcomed with open arms as shipwrecked mariners and, for the payment of one shilling each, we were made life members of the local coal miner's union. We had great difficulty in rescuing Pongo from the arms of one of the local damsels and eventually returned to our bunks though not without further mishap as Hutch (Flight Lieutenant Hutchins) missed the gang plank and fell into the harbour, thereby sobering him up completely.

CHAPTER 4

The Blenheim

Empire day in May saw the squadron scattered over England as Blenheims were still the latest and best bomber in the RAF and one went to each RAF station open to the public. I took one over to my previous station in Berkshire to which my family had travelled down for the display. After a slow fly past at 90 mph with undercarriage and flaps down, in contrast, I did another run across the airfield at 250 mph and landed and taxied to the site where many types were on display. Late in the afternoon, all aircraft took-off again to return to their respective stations and I flew blind back home, and back to Maureen.

At the beginning of July, the squadron again moved to the armament practice camp in Dorset for three weeks' training but, as with our Blenheims, we were only allowed to do bombing, life was not so strenuous as at previous camps. Practice with the guns was out, as it was considered that the aircraft was too fast and too heavy to be safe to use against ground targets and the drogue towing aircraft was too slow. So all available time was spent in high level and low level bombing. Despite being in the middle of summer, we had foul weather which considerably curtailed flying.

For pilots who were used to open cockpits and a fixed undercarriage the Blenheim, with its complicated hydraulics systems, was something of a challenge. It was a lot faster than anything most pilots had flown before and it had a cruising speed of 266 mph at 14,000 feet. The RAF lost 10 per cent of its Blenheims in flying accidents before the war began and a number of accidents were caused by pilots forgetting to put the wheels down.

62 Squadron lost its first Blenheim on 8 November 1938 when L116, flown by Sergeant Bannell, stalled while flying over Luce Bay, a danger area in Wigtownshire that is still used as a bombing range. The aircraft lost flying speed and began to jink as the throttles were pulled back and its pilot made a forced landing on the beach with the undercarriage retracted. The AOC blamed 'Faulty Flying' but subsequent similar incidents suggest that it may have been a technical failure.

During the camp, I flew up to group headquarters in company with half a dozen other officers from the squadron to take promotion examination 'A' to qualify for promotion to flying officer. This examination consisted of drilling a squadron, the Morse code on the buzzer and Aldis lamp, and oral tests in administration, flying and engines. We were told unofficially that we had all passed and so we returned to camp happy in the knowledge that another milestone had been passed.

On our return to camp, we took part in an extensive exercise on a war footing. This confined us all to camp for several days and crews slept in the hangars at instant readiness. We flew many quadroon sorties into the North Sea, returning and 'bombing' some of the larger cities. Then the whole squadron packed up and went on three weeks' leave, except the adjutant. I thought it would be a good time in which to catch up on the paper work in preparation for the 'P' staff inspection in the autumn. And, of course, I was not completely alone as Maureen was only seven miles away.

At the beginning of September, our CO was relieved by a much younger squadron leader, a first class officer we quickly learned to admire and respect. I was kept extremely busy with the administrative work, but the new congenial atmosphere made things so much easier. The past fourteen months had been very trying at times and, although I gave my CO complete loyalty, one could not help on occasions despising his methods.

The new CO was Squadron Leader Geoff Farnhill. He had previously been the 'B' Flight commander to which Harley belonged and he took over command from Squadron Leader J.C.E.A. Johnson on 12 September 1938.

It had been obvious that our training to bring the squadron to operational efficiency had been pushed ahead with all speed, but now it became even more intensive with long cross-country flights and a series of endurance trials to ascertain the range of the Blenheim at varying heights and speeds. The atmosphere was tense and we waited for the balloon to go up.

At the beginning of November, half the squadron flew up to an armament training camp in Scotland. A few days later I followed. It was a delightful trip, via the Isle of Man, but with an ignominious ending. Arriving over the aerodrome, it appeared to be completely water-logged but, having permission to land, I chose the best line to avoid the miniature lake and landed. The aerodrome was quite small and, when I applied the brakes, the wheels just locked and skidded through mud without reducing the speed of the aircraft. In a few seconds, the buildings started to loom up in front of me.

I tried to swing the aircraft but without success as the ground was too soft to offer any grip, and I crashed into the duty pilot's office, hitting it with my port wing. The hut, being of wooden construction, was demolished. The tail of the aircraft swung round and crashed into the fire tender, at the same time breaking the fuselage clean in two aft of the wireless operator. None of my crew was injured but the aircraft looked a sorry mess and I was not at all pleased with myself – a £30,000 Blenheim written off.

This incident happened on 14 November 1938 at West Freugh near Stranraer when Blenheim, L1108, was badly damaged and broke its back, just behind the gun turret. The accident car (Form 1180) states that, 'The aircraft overshot the runway and the brakes were ineffective because of muddy ground.'

The crash had all the potential of a very serious life threatening accident but it did have its funny side, although Harley did probably not appreciate that at the time. The story that went around claimed that the duty pilot was not expecting the arrival of another aircraft and he was on the toilet when Harley was made his approach to land. If that was true he must have had quite a shock when he was interrupted by the noise that the Blenheim made when it hit the building.

The following month, on 12 December, Harley was promoted to the rank of flying officer and shortly afterwards his service was extended to six years.

To my intense relief, I was exonerated from all blame at the subsequent Court of Inquiry – it appeared that an aerodrome Unserviceability Signal had not been sent out – but it did not help very much my own chagrin at the loss of one of our aircraft.

1938 drew to a close. I was presented to the AOC at his annual inspection 'for proficiency in duties' – a minor honour granted to the few – and I received my promotion to flying officer. With the happy thought of my driving licence being restored to me in January I went home to my people for the Christmas festivities. (It is not known exactly when and for what Harley lost his licence.)

On my return from Christmas leave, I was greeted with the news that we were again off to the armament training camp for three weeks and so I elected to drive the 160 miles, taking with me my flight sergeant and all the necessary squadron records. It was a most enjoyable run, especially after my six months' penance. Practically every evening during the winter months I had run the engine of the car, so that it was in perfect trim. It went like a bomb.

We did practically no flying the first week as we had almost continuous rain and the coast was lashed by heavy gales and blizzards. But we made the most of the fair periods and this time, in addition to bombing, the air gunners were allowed to get in some air firing practice on the drogue. On our return to home base we again took part in extensive air exercises, joining up with several squadrons and coming in from the North Sea for high level 'bombing' attacks on several of the large manufacturing centres in the north of England. We were kept very busy these days and, in addition, we flew at night whenever the weather permitted, on long navigational exercises and practise bombing on the local range.

I had a few days leave at home in the middle of March but was recalled by telegram, thanks to the uneasy international situation created by Mr Hitler. All personnel were confined to camp and I was fully occupied with revising the squadron's mobilization scheme, as we were earmarked to move to France at the outbreak of hostilities.

We had our first fatal accident in the squadron when one of our aircraft did not return from a navigational flight. One of our young officers and his crew crashed in bad weather, killing all three. Such fatalities naturally created a depression in the squadron and aircrews were reminded how near they lived to death. It is hardly to be wondered that this type of mortal appreciates and enjoys life more, and lives it to the full.

This accident happened on 22 March when Blenheim L1262 crashed at Cranford, near Kettering in Northamptonshire. The tragedy was not caused by the result of any technical failure but probably as a result of the severe weather conditions and the fact that the aircraft had flown through a particularly bad hailstorm. The three crew, which consisted of Pilot Officer Shine, navigator, Sergeant Wiles and air gunner Aircraftman Lewis, were all killed in the initial impact.

62 Squadron got off to a bad start in 1939 and Harley does not mention another accident that happened on 10 January involving Pilot Officer Owensmiths, who was flying L1114. He was reducing power to land, when one of the Bristol Mercury engines cut out and he had to make a forced landing in a field near Granmoor. He was not seriously injured and no blame was put on the pilot who was flying on a cross-country exercise in East Yorkshire at the time. The accident card states that, 'Second engine failed, no fault of pilot'.

In April, after two years in the job, I handed over my duties as adjutant and was posted to 'B' Flight where I could anticipate a lot more flying. But I was not allowed much leisure even then. The Air Cadet Corps came into being, to provide preliminary training for the youth of Britain who were keen on flying and who might, at some later date, join the Royal Air Force. I had been on a selection board, sorting out young men for Air Force, Army or Navy training and I was now appointed liaison officer with No. 5 Air Defence Cadet Squadron, Northampton, and my squadron was officially affiliated to the City of Northampton.

So every Thursday night was spent with these young boys, giving them an insight into the organization and activities of the service and for whom I arranged various lectures by specialist officers. It was all very interesting and I think they enjoyed being in contact with the regular Air Force, and my encouragement was amply rewarded by their eager enthusiasm.

At this time I was also working on the arrangements for a squadron reunion dinner and was busy tracking down all the old First World War members. As far as I could ascertain, there was only one of the original members still serving, a wing commander who was commanding a station in Yorkshire. I flew up there and had lunch with him. The information he gave me of the old squadron was most interesting and, in parting, he presented me with the altimeter off a German machine which he had shot down in 1917 together with a photograph of the officers of the squadron taken in France. These gifts were highly appreciated; the altimeter was suitably mounted, the photograph framed and both were placed in the Mess.

62 Squadron had originally been formed at Filton near Bristol on 8 August 1916 and during the First World War it had flown various versions of the Be 2, Avro 504 and the Bristol Fighter. It lost a total of twenty airmen killed in the service of the Royal Flying Corps and another twenty-four who died after the formation of the Royal Air Force.

What Harley probably did not know was that an airman bearing his surname had served on 62 Squadron and had been killed on 28 March 1918. He was Air Mechanic 1st Class Albert Boxall (23399) and as far as we know the two men were not related. Harley's family was from the Midlands while Albert's family lived in Highbury, north London.

It appeared that the old squadron had never been granted an official badge, a squadron crest, so we set about devising one. From an inspiration of my father's, I designed a badge which, after going through the College of Heralds and approval by the King, was subsequently presented to the squadron by the AOC, Bomber Group. We also had a tie made by Gieves which incorporated the emblem.

Relieved of my administrative duties, I spent most of my time in the air. For a week, in order to take advantage of the weather, we worked from 1200 to 0200 the following morning to get in as much night flying as possible. It was about this time that I learned that I had been recommended for a permanent commission irrespective of the results of the specialization examination which we normally had to pass. This was a tremendous piece of news for me, as I was getting a little worried about this examination, and it spurred me on to greater efforts.

In May we held the squadron reunion dinner at the RAF Club in Piccadilly. Apart from the present officers, we had nine of the old members with us. Some of them had not seen each other since the beginning of the Armistice; and the last one saw of another was when he was going down in flames. It was a memorable evening and many were the experiences exchanged between the old and the new. The party broke up in the early hours having forged a link between the old squadron with its Bristol Fighters and the present with its modern bomber.

The summer of 1939 will always be remembered as one of extraordinary good weather, despite the war clouds gathering in Europe. England was beautiful and, without doubt, they were the happiest days of my life. I was completely happy in my work with many good friends and a little car that was a joy to drive which took me to my darling London most weekends. Life was wonderful.

Time passed very quickly. We were at home to the public on Empire Day in May when we put on the usual flying display. I took over the part-time duties of the Mess secretary that had the advantage of relieving me from the duty of orderly officer and, in June, we entertained over 100 members of the Observer Corps, explaining the workings of the station and acting as 'bus drivers' on local flights in the afternoon.

In July, we spent an enjoyable day on a destroyer watching aircraft bombing HMS *Centurion* – a target battleship. There was rather an amusing episode in the ward room before lunch when the Navy was plying us with gin. I was sitting on an ordinary chair when the destroyer changed direction at full speed, heeling over in the process. Without noticing it, the centrifugal force had lifted the front legs of the chair off the deck and I was serenely balanced on the rear legs only. Unfortunately for the good name of the RAF, the turn got tighter and I overbalanced flat on my back. In spite of the jibes at not being able to hold my gin, I still maintain that I was the only one on that ship who maintained a perpendicular position during that manoeuvre.

At the end of July, I went home on a week's leave but, true to form, I had a telegram from the adjutant after a couple of days instructing me to return. This I did, wondering what the 'flap' was about this time. On my arrival I was met with the exciting news that the squadron had been posted to Singapore, and was leaving the next month. This was tremendous, as we had often wondered whether we should ever get overseas, and the fact that the whole squadron was going as a unit made it even more delightful. The ground crews were leaving by sea in a few weeks time and we were to fly out our aircraft in August.

I handed over the Mess secretary-ship and resumed the duties of adjutant. Many additional personnel arrived to make up the squadron establishment. Movement orders were drawn up and all the squadron equipment was being packed. On top of this, we had to get measured for tropical kit, which necessitated a pleasant few hours in London. Cars had to be disposed of at the best price possible – my little Minx (Harley owned at least four makes of car at different times) fetched only £35. All the squadron personnel had to be inoculated, kitted up and packed off on embarkation leave. Ground crews were busy on our twelve aircraft making them ready for our long flight to the other side of the world.

I was able to get a few days leave at home to say goodbye to my family and friends and returned in time for our farewell party in the Mess. We must have had 100 guests, including all the local people who had shown us so much hospitality and, although we were looking forward with eagerness to our new life in the Far East, our gaiety was tinged with a certain sadness at leaving this station at which we had spent such happy times during the past two years.

Maureen came up for the party and stayed in the local town until the morning of my departure. In the last few days we spent all our free time together, hanging on to the last moments of our happiness. At the final parting, we struggled to hold back our tears but I think we both knew that we should never see each other again.

CHAPTER 5

An Epic Journey

By the outbreak of war the RAF had more Blenheims than any other type of aircraft with 1,089 on the strength of its squadrons. The first Blenheims to serve overseas were those of 30 Squadron that had been re-equipped while it was based at Habbaniya in Iraq. Those aircraft had been stripped down by a special unit based at RAF Sealand and, during late 1937, they were shipped out in huge packing cases. The squadron eventually received its first aircraft in January 1938.

During the summer of 1939 and because of increasing political tension in Europe, a decision was taken to reinforce the Far East Air Force with two squadrons of Blenheims. The urgency of the situation required that the aircraft, from 34 and 62 Squadrons, be flown out to their final destination at Tengah in Singapore. The ground party, administrative personnel and surplus aircrew left Cranfield on 12 August and sailed to Singapore on HMT *Nautilus*.

Today a modern airliner like a Boeing 747 can fly from Britain to Singapore non-stop in just under 13 hours but in 1939 it took the Blenheims nearly three weeks. Although Harley mentions the strength of each flight being six aircraft, there were actually eight Blenheims in both flights, with 'A' Flight departing on 23 August. Harley's 'B' Flight took off three days later at 1200.

One flight of Blenheims from 34 Squadron based at Watton had left for Singapore on the 16th and a second followed on 19 August. 62 Squadron followed the same route. Exact details about the progress of individual aircraft and crews are not available and the official records only give an overall account of 62 Squadron's journey to the Far East.

We left England on the 27 August 1939. 'A' Flight with six aircraft had left two days before, as the airfields en route could not accommodate the whole squadron at one time. We took-off in two sections of three and joined up in flight formation over the airfield. I took one last look at our station below and then brought my aircraft close up in formation on the leader.

We were soon over the English Channel and crossing the coastline into France. The weather was good and, after some hours flying, Marseilles came into view. Forming line astern, we landed and were immediately caught up in the boisterous hospitality of the French Air Force. They seemed to think that, being English, all we required was beer and whisky whereas we were all feeling the pangs of hunger. However not wishing to offend the French officers in any way, we dealt with their drinks and then proceeded in taxis to the city. After a meal I went straight to bed as I had a splitting headache; but from some of the experiences that were related the following morning, I seemed to have missed quite a lot of fun.

The following morning we left Marseilles on the long sea crossing to Malta. Skirting the top of Sicily, the island appeared through the haze and we landed at the RAF airfield. In the evening, we had a delightful swim in the blue Mediterranean and a quiet evening in the Mess before retiring.

Two aircraft from 62 Squadron, one from each flight, became unserviceable while on the ground at Marseilles and they and their crews had to be left behind. Not all aircraft made it even as far as Malta and a Blenheim, from 34 Squadron, L8378, crashed into the sea, some seventy miles south-east of Sicily. The crew were not seriously injured and were picked up by a French fishing boat.

Although Harley mentions Mersah Matruh as being in Libya, it was actually in Egypt, some sixty miles east of Sidi Barrani. Designated LG 08 it was one of a number of landing grounds that were situated close to the coast, but less than 100 miles north of the notorious Qattara Depression.

Off at dawn the next day for the 800 mile flight across the sea to Libya, where we landed at Mersah Matruh, an advanced RAF landing ground. The landing area was defined solely by empty petrol tins and with the visibility being almost nil, there were one or two exciting moments dodging stray camels. We had to refuel here out of four-gallon petrol tins, which was quite a lengthy business as each aircraft required well over 100 gallons and, although the storm had abated somewhat, we had to take every precaution to ensure that no sand got into the petrol.

We had lunch at a most luxurious hotel on the shores of the Mediterranean and a quick dip where Cleopatra is said to have bathed. Then off for the trip to Heliopolis, on the outskirts of Cairo, which was to be our night stop. With the coastline always in view, we passed the Pyramids of Giza and landed at Heliopolis. We had a couple of days there, which gave us the opportunity of looking around the capital of Egypt, a city of palatial buildings and abject slums. The pungent smell assailed our nostrils, an odour which in varying degrees pervaded our lives for the next few years.

We left Egypt and set course for Habbaniyah in Iraq, across Palestine, Transjordan and Oman. The weather was fine except for a heat haze through which could largely be discerned the barren waste of the countries below. On landing the heat was so intense that, within a few minutes, it was impossible to touch the surface of the aircraft. Habbaniyah was a real outpost of the Empire, a military town surrounded by defences, set in the heart of the desert. All the amenities were there to make life bearable; swimming pools, sports grounds and comfortable accommodation, but we were not sorry to leave after one night's stay.

As Harley's 'B' Flight was approaching Sharjah, the seven remaining Blenheims of 'A' Flight were already on the ground at Karachi. By comparison, the steamship *Nautilus*, which was carrying ground crew and equipment, was an estimated three days away from arriving in Colombo, Ceylon.

But worse was to follow when, the next day we took-off for Sharjah at the southern end of the Persian Gulf. The heat haze obscured the lifeless desert. From the air, the clear waters of the Gulf showed mighty chasms in the depth, very forbidding and, as we knew, very shark-ridden. We landed on the smooth sand at Sharjah and pegged down our aircraft for the night. The local sheikh provided a guard of twenty men, a more ferocious looking lot I had yet to see, bearing rifles and bristling with knives. We bathed in the river, but it was just like getting into a hot bath. We all moved into the fort at sundown and heavy gates were bolted and barred to keep out the local brigands. The heat was so intense even after the sun had gone down that we ate our dinner in the courtyard with just a towel around our loins and perspiration rolled of as though we were under a shower bath. There was very little sleep that night and we were glad to leave at dawn on our journey over Afghanistan for our next halt at Karachi on the north-west coast of India.

We landed at RAF Station Drigh Road, east of the city and it was like returning to civilization again. This was one of the oldest RAF Stations in India, with solid stone buildings and an atmosphere of hospitality engendered by years of tradition. It was a very comfortable station and the Mess, with its Hindu and Muslim bearers, was exceptionally well run.

It was 3 September. In the evening we were invited to the Karachi Swimming Club. This was one of the European clubs, set on piles above the waters of the Indus. It was very pleasant sitting out there on the balcony in the tropical night, with shaded lights and soft music played by Indian bands. At 2000 the BBC news came through and everything was hushed. We heard the Prime Minister give the electrifying news that we were at war with Germany and before we could vent our emotions the National Anthem brought us to our feet to attention.

Then the place was in an uproar. It was impossible to appreciate the true import of this astounding news, especially by most of us sat at the table who had been too young to remember the destruction and suffering of the First World War. I do not think that any of us thought that the alarms of the past year would lead to war really breaking out. And yet, in some way it was a relief from the tension under which we had been living. Our immediate consideration was what was going to happen to us. Here we were, half way to Singapore, when we knew that the fun was going to start in Europe. Without doubt, we must return and take our place. This is what we had been training for, for three years. It was annoying to think that the squadron we had left behind at Cranfield would be in the mêlée before us. We could not help but think of the families we had left behind in Britain who, even now, might be subject to bombardment by the enemy. The whole situation was fantastic, and the arguments went on into the night.

We eagerly awaited the decision of the Air Ministry and after a few hours it came through. We were to go on to Singapore. Since leaving Egypt I had been suffering constant tummy trouble and running a temperature and, as we were due to stay in Karachi for a few days, I went to the Military Hospital where they diagnosed sand-fly fever. I responded quickly to treatment, greatly assisted by my own desire not to get left behind. Even so, the onward flight had to be postponed for a day until I was pronounced fit.

Three Blenehims of 'B' Flight had already taken-off from Karachi on 8 September but four aircraft, including Harley's, stayed behind. Another two followed on a few days later but Harley and one other crew remained there until he was well enough to travel. On the 9th a ship carrying the sea party of six officers, twelve NCOs and 110 airmen arrived in Singapore.

We took-off at dawn and set course for Allahabad. Up until then, we had been very fortunate with the weather but now, across India, we ran into the monsoon. It was actually the worst time of the year for flying in this part of the world, and the further east we went the worse it become. It was difficult to avoid these formidable storms as they covered such a vast area, and the meteorological information was completely unreliable. On the horizon, the storms ahead presented a black wall of torrential rain, electrified by lightning flashes. Try as we might to circumvent it, more often than not we had to go through.

To attempt to climb above the storm was usually abortive as the cumulus cloud often reached to 25, 000 feet or more. So we closed in tight formation and went in. It was almost like diving into the sea. The rain was so terrific that it was barely possible to see the leader, and then only as a blur through the streaming perspex. Great up-currents tossed the aircraft 100 feet and then, just as suddenly, smacked it down. One literally had to fight the machine to keep it on an even keel. The blackness, pierced by flashes of lightning, was turning it into a dirty yellow, then the darkness enveloped us again. After what seemed like an interminable time the storm abated, the sky became lighter and we broke through into the sunlight once more.

On the way we had breakfast at Jodhpur, and finally landed at Allahabad, a civil aerodrome. Here we kicked our heels for eight days as the flight preceding ours was held up at Calcutta by persistent bad weather. We stayed in the Mess of the Queen's Royal Regiment and I think the boisterous RAF upset their sedate way of life. We had plenty of time to explore the city of Allahabad, set on the banks of the Ganges.

Harley was to return to Jodphur a few years later in a totally different capacity and the city was to play an important part in his life, as was India generally. 'A' Flight remained on the ground at Calcutta for eight days before it finally departed for Akyab on 14 September. When its seven Blenheims landed there it was found that one aircraft had a burnt exhaust ring, while another two had faulty instruments. Four aircraft left Akyab on 15 September, but the other three remained there awaiting repairs.

The five Blenheims of 'B' Flight landed at Calcutta on the 16th and refuelled before they departed for Rangoon a few hours later. On the same day the first four Blenehims of 'A' Flight arrived at Alor Star in Malaya and after refuelling continued on to Mergui. Two of the three Blenheims from 'A' Flight that proved to be unserviceable when they landed at Akyab also left for Rangoon on the 16th, while the third aircraft left on its own the next day.

At last we were able to get away and, through rain storms, arrived at Calcutta where we refuelled our aircraft. Then out across the Indian Ocean to Burma. It was a stormy passage and we flew all the way a few feet above the waves. At last land appeared through the rain and we set down safely at Rangoon.

We received a friendly welcome from the Gloucester Regiment with whom we stayed and, in the evening, a young lieutenant took me into the city twelve miles away. This was my first night out since leaving England and, having fully recovered from the fever, we made the most of it.

The Middle East and India – what little we had seen of these places – had not evoked any great interest, in fact our first impressions of life overseas left us a little disappointed. But when we arrived at Rangoon, the first mystic enchantment of the Far East steeped into our blood; the people, cleaner and in a higher state of civilization, more physically attractive and seemingly more honest, were of a much better type than the races with whom we had come in brief contact in the last few weeks. The country, with its lush vegetation, was such a pleasant relief from the arid barrenness of the deserts over which we had flown.

The young lieutenant obviously knew his way around Rangoon and was good company. We sampled all the cabarets, with their soft music and dusky dance hostesses, and finally finished up at five in the morning eating roast chicken at a native stall – in accordance with the local custom.

We arrived back in the Mess in time for morning tea. I had a quick shower and we took-off at 0630 for Mergui. This hop was probably the worst throughout the entire journey. We flew at 18,000 feet, slipping between the cumulus cloud which even at that height towered above us. Having missed breakfast, I sustained myself with oxygen and malted milk tablets. Eventually, after some searching, we caught a glimpse of the landing ground through a gap in the clouds. Putting the aircraft into almost a vertical dive, so as not to lose sight of our temporary haven, we screamed down to earth and landed.

On 18 September the five Blenheims of 'B' Flight flew from Rangoon to Mergui, on the western peninsula of Siam where they were delayed by bad weather. The other two Blenheims of 'B' Flight, one of them being Harley's aircraft, also flew from Rangoon to Mergui, where they were held up by bad weather. At 1430 on the same day four Blenheims of 'A' Flight arrived at RAF Tengah. It had taken them a total of 50 flying hours to get there.

For one crew the sector between Mergui and Alor Star proved too much and L1139, flown by Flying Officer Powell, made a forced landing in the jungle at Trang in Siam after he got lost. The aircraft was a total write-off but fortunately none of the crew was seriously injured. The other three airmen on board were Sergeant Walker, LAC Blewitt and LAC Hicks.

Mergui was a hole cut out of the jungle, surrounded by very high trees on all sides so that the landing was not easy. However, we all got down safely and refuelled. Within the hour we were airborne, hoping to make Singapore that day. But the weather was so bad, and having lost time and fuel in trying to dodge the worst storms, we landed at Alor Star, 400 miles from Singapore.

Alor Star – what a pretty name – was the capital of the un- federated State of Kedah, in the north of Malaya. Set in idyllic surroundings, encompassed by paddy fields it was to become the focal point for three major episodes in my life. The following day it poured with rain so we delayed our departure. Clearing late in the afternoon, we went into Alor Star nine miles away, and had our first view of a Malayan town.

The following morning, we left at dawn for the short hop to Singapore. After 1 hour 30 minutes flying, the island at the tip came into view and then, skirting the prohibited area of the Naval base, we saw the hangars of Tengah aerodrome, our destination. We shot up the aerodrome and landed, to be welcomed by the rest of the squadron and our ground crews who had arrived by sea some days before.

The first four Blenheims of 'B' Flight landed at Tengah on the 19th while the remaining two aircraft of 'A' Flight did not arrive until the 22nd. 'B' Flight's three remaining Blenheims had a rather disruptive time during the last couple of sectors but Harley's aircraft and one other landed on the 23rd. The third aircraft of 'B' Flight was forced to land at Penang because of bad weather but flew on to Tengah the next day.

HMT *Nautilus* had arrived in Singapore on the 21st but the SS *Protesilians* which carried most of 62 Squadron's ground equipment did not dock until the 23rd. It took two days to offload and transport the equipment to Tenghah.

It was hard to believe that we had really come to the end of our journey, we had been wandering over the face of the earth so long. It was three weeks since we left Cranfield, although the actual flying time was only 40 hours for the 8,000 mile journey. We had flown over a dozen countries, to a strange airfield for each landing, experiencing for the first time the heat of the desert, the menace of the impenetrable jungles and the violence of the tropical weather which was to be our medium for the next two years.

CHAPTER 6

RAF Tengah

The British defences of Singapore were established in the nineteenth century with the building of a number of forts on the southern coast. The first of these was Fort Fullerton, which was established in 1830 and it was followed by Fort Canning in 1853. The last defensive position on this model was Fort Slinsing that was built in 1901.

The RAF's presence in Singapore had its origins in a decision taken by the Government in 1923, when it was chosen as the site for a new naval base and an air station was established at Seletar to provide local air defence. Seletar was a grass strip airfield with a 3,000 feet runway that boasted an engine repair unit and facilities to house up to three squadrons.

RAF Tengah was built in 1937 on the western side of Singapore in between two mangrove swamps that were situated to the north and east. It was a grass airfield with two runways, one measuring approximately 2,800 feet and the other 2,400 feet long. It had two large hangars and the only previous residents were 11 and 27 Squadrons. 27 was a training unit equipped with Tiger Moths. That unit was moved out to India shortly after 62 Squadron arrived.

As 34 Squadron arrived in Singapore just ahead of 62 Squadron, its personnel probably got the first choice of accommodation and maintenance facilities. Inspections of 62 Squadron's aircraft revealed that the epic journey from England, and the minimum of a dozen landings on desert strips and jungle clearances, had caused a huge amount of wear and tear. It was also discovered for the first time that there was a severe shortage of spare parts for the Bristol Mercury engines and other major components.

One of the first operations involving 62 Squadron was a paper training exercise for air observers that was carried out in the station's operation room. They were given maps to understand the local geography and were instructed in search and reconnaissance procedures and cooperation with the Royal Navy. This meant that they had to learn about naval codes, sea charts, lighthouses, the most regularly used sea lanes and local landmarks.

Not all of 62 Squadron's pilots had flown out to Singapore and a small number of the less experienced had sailed there. By the time they arrived they had not flown for several weeks and local refresher flights were organized to familiarize them both with the Blenheim and the local area. Two formations of aircraft were detailed for cooperation work with the guns and searchlight batteries in Singapore and these aircraft carried out the city's first air defence exercise. This involved mock high level air attacks on the city's floating dock and Union Building.

The first impressions of our new home were excellent. The station, 14 miles from Singapore, had actually been cut out of a rubber plantation and it had been built as a peacetime station, in other words all the buildings were of solid construction. It appeared that no expense had been spared to make life as comfortable and congenial as possible for the men who were to spend their two-and-a-half year tour of duty in this part of the far flung Empire. The two storey barrack blocks were light and airy, well equipped with hot and cold water laid on for showers and baths, and modern sanitation throughout.

The station boasted its own swimming pool and tennis courts and the roads throughout the camp were wide and well made. The airfield itself was grass covered, but later a concrete runway was made to ensure that it was serviceable for aircraft in all weathers. There were two large hangars, one of which housed the squadron's aircraft and, shortly afterwards, another Blenheim squadron arrived and took over the second.

On our arrival, the Officer's Mess was not yet ready for occupation and so, for the first four months, we lived in Warrant Officer's married quarters, four officers sharing the house and feeding in another which had been converted into a temporary Mess.

I think we were all somewhat enervated by the change in climate but, strangely enough, although we were only eighty miles from the equator, the weather was never particularly hot – nothing like the temperatures of Egypt or Iraq – just a steady 80 – 85 degrees every day. But at these temperatures, with a steady humidity around the 90 per cent mark, one was always in a state of unpleasant 'stickiness' and the general thundery atmosphere had a soporific effect.

After a few weeks one got used to it to a certain extent. But, at the beginning, most of us used to retire for a short nap after lunch.

We soon got into our daily routine: at 0630 we rose and were put through 15 minutes' physical training then a quick shower and into breakfast by 0700. A pleasant walk across the airfield and we were in the Flights at 0730. For the first 90 minutes we attended lectures if we were not on early flying, then into the air on some navigation or bombing practice. We packed up at 1230 after a hard day's work.

Soon after our arrival at Tengah I had handed back the duties of adjutant but was immediately saddled with the job of squadron censor officer. As we were now on active service all outgoing private mail had to be censored, and it was a boring and unpleasant job reading other people's letters, scoring out anything that might have been of value to an enemy in the event of these letters falling into their hands. As was to be expected, the volume of correspondence on a Monday morning was staggering and fortunately other jobs came my way within a short time which relieved me of this irritating task.

A flight of three aircraft was always kept on standby duties in readiness for enemy shipping appearing in these eastern waters. But when we were not thus confined to camp, we spent the afternoons and evenings in Singapore. The attraction in the afternoon was the Swimming Club which was delightful and must have been one of the best in the world, apart from providing the most pleasant form of recreation and exercise in this climate. Then we would either go to a cinema with modern air-conditioning or enjoy an excellent meal at one of the hotels or cafes. The city of Singapore was enchanting.

Enjoyment of this overseas station was naturally tempered by the Armageddon raging in Europe. In normal times our two-and-a-half years' tour of duty of the Far East would have been an enviable experience, but ever present thought of the impending blow on our families and friends in Britain gave cause for much private anxiety which was not assuaged in the least by the knowledge that we, out here in Singapore, seemed condemned to remain in idleness and safety whilst our comrades were, even now, carrying the war to the enemy's territory.

Soon after it arrived at Tengah, 62 Squadron was informed that the two aircraft that had been left behind at Marseilles had been removed from the unit's strength, together with their crews. To make matters worse, on 2 October two more aircraft were damaged after the airfield was flooded by heavy rain and their undercarriage and flaps were swamped on landing. There was good news on 4 October when Flying Officer Powell and his crew from 'A' Flight were reunited with the squadron at Tengah. The Siamese Government had eventually allowed them to leave the country and they travelled to Singapore by train.

The squadron was also boosted by the arrival of Sergeant

Geoffrey William Haigh, who was posted in from No. 4 Anti-Aircraft Cooperation Unit at Seletar. He was a former airline pilot who had flown with Wearn's Airways in Australia and, because of his considerable flying experience, would soon be commissioned. The 33 year old was originally from Britain but had spent much of his life in Australia.

The air mail service was disrupted on 27 August 1939 when France prohibited flights over certain parts of its territory and similar restrictions were imposed over Sardinia, Sicily, Italy and the Italian-occupied Dodecanese Islands. In September Imperial Airways moved its base from Southampton to Poole and a new air mail service began on 7 September.

Our anxiety was accentuated by the lack of news from home. Immediately after the outbreak of hostilities the air mail service had been suspended and it was over a month after our arrival that letters began to trickle in by sea mail. Fortunately, within a few weeks the air mail service was re-started and then continued with comforting regularity. But the disquieting news of air raids over Britain and the appearance of the first casualty list, in which the names of two of my friends from training days had already appeared, compelled me to apply for a posting to the Home Establishment for service with the RAF in the field, as did several other members of my squadron.

Naturally we could only view the times from our own personal points of view. The grand strategy and the politico-military appreciation of the trend of events in the Far East were unknown to us. Our impression was that the war would be confined to Europe and that it would soon be over, and the last thing we wanted was to stagnate in Singapore when, it seemed to us, all our squadrons should be thrown into the battle.

Fortunately for my peace of mind, and within three weeks of my arrival in Singapore, I was sent up into the north of Malaya on a special job, to investigate the practical ability of operating Blenheim aircraft from the landing ground at Kota Bharu. This was in the north-east of Malaya in the un-federated State of Kelantan, ten miles from the border with Siam (Thailand). I had a busy morning at air headquarters being briefed for my mission and left Singapore by the night train. The 400 mile journey took 20 hours and was quite comfortable in the air-conditioned train, spotlessly clean with good meals.

I was met at Kota Bharu station by the contractor, Monty, who was responsible for the upkeep of the landing ground, a gentleman whose main livelihood was the processing and marketing of copra, the dried meat of the coconut. He took me home to his luxurious bungalow and I stayed with him for a few days until the accommodation at the landing ground was ready for occupation.

Kota Bharu was quite a large town with a population of over 15,000 people and it was the capital of the province of Kelentan, situated close to the border of Siam (Thailand). Harley's orders were as a result of Operational Order No. 1, dated 10 October 1939, which was concerned with the assessment of airfields in Malaya for their use by the Blenheim. Other airfields at Batu Pahat, Port Swettenham and Sitiawan were to be categorized for their use at night, in an emergency and whether they could be used by fully laden aircraft or those only lightly loaded.

To add to the complicated formula an assessment had to be made, as to whether or not each airfield could be used by both experienced and inexperienced pilots in the various categories. An experienced pilot was classed as one who had completed 500 hours solo with at least 50 of them on the Blenheim. A pilot might also be considered experienced, if he had 100 hours on the Blenheim, with at least 10 of them flown at night.

Kelantan was still very much a native state, ruled under a feudal system by the Sultan with the assistance of His Majesty's representative, the British Resident. There were very few Europeans and, except for a handful of planters, they were all colonial service officials. My host lived comfortably in his spacious bungalow, with soft-footed Malay servants to gratify every want. True to the old traditions, he dressed for dinner every evening and the meal was served with great decorum, accompanied by a bottle of champagne in which I duly assisted him.

The following morning we went out to the landing ground a few miles distant. It was an open area, cut out of the jungle, roughly rectangular in shape. With Monty's assistance, I took the dimensions and found that one direction would give the necessary length for a Blenheim to land and take-off. Fortunately this was in line with the prevailing wind but the approaches at either end had to be cleared further back to reduce the angle of descent. I marked out the landing area and arranged with Monty for several depressions to be filled in by the coolies to improve the surface.

Then we inspected the living accommodation, set in one corner of the landing ground, which was practically ready for occupation. During the next two days, I supervised the furnishing of these 'Basha' huts, arranged with a Chinese contractor to do the catering, brought in the required stocks of petrol and oil and arranged with the commissioner of Kelantan police for an aircraft guard. When all was ready, I dispatched a telegram to AHQ giving the relevant information on the landing ground with the best (and only) directions in which to land. The following day, two of our Blenheims arrived and landed safely.

One of the Blenheims belonged to 62 Squadron, while the other was from 11 Squadron and they made the first ever landing on the 3,600 feet runway at Kota Bharu during the morning of Saturday 14 October. The 62 Squadron Blenheim was flown by the CO, Squadron Leader Farnhill and the aircraft from 11 Squadron by Flight Lieutenant Dudgeon. The two aircraft remained at Kota Bharu until Wednesday the 18th and both the pilots and crews had been ordered by Air HQ to be courteous and take the local dignitaries for flights, as and when requested.

The airfield at Kota Bharu came out of the assessment quite well and it only failed in a couple of categories involving operations flown at night, by both experienced and inexperienced pilots. In the struggle that followed the Japanese invasion it was to become an important and strategic airfield.

During our stay, we did a fair amount of flying and gave 'joy rides' to most of the local Government officials and their wives. They were a most hospitable crowd and one afternoon they entertained us to a 'curry tiffin' at a marvellous beach at Backok, some thirty-five miles by road south of Kota Bharu. It was a perfect tropical setting, a wonderful stretch of fine white sand as far as the eye could see, with coconut trees stretching down to the water's edge and the sea rolling in gently on the shore.

This was the weekend resort of the local Europeans. They had built several beach huts and, bringing their own servants with them from Kota Bharu, they whiled away the hours of rest in idyllic surroundings. The curry lunch provided was stupendous and it was rather surprising to me that they could put away so much of it helped down by quantities of cold beer. No wonder most of them retired to sleep in the afternoon but, for myself, having a small appetite, I made the most of this delightful spot, swimming and exploring the beach. I was intrigued by the methods used by Malay fishermen. They would wade into the water and throw their nets into the air which, opening like parachutes, literally fell over the shoals of small fish which were in abundance.

The following evening we were invited to a cocktail dance at the British Residency where we met many of the local nobility, sultans, princes and rajahs, but their ladies, being of the Mohammedan faith, were kept out of sight. This seclusion only applied to the noble women. In the town and in the 'kampong' (villages) the women went unveiled and mixed freely. They were most attractive creatures, small in build but exceedingly proportioned, very pretty in their multi-coloured sarongs and bajus. With their light brown skin, rounded features and soft dark eyes, it was not to be wondered at, that most of the single white men living in isolation from their own folk succumbed to their charms and took them as mistresses.

After five days the two aircraft returned to Tengah and, after closing the camp

Acting Pilot Officer Harley Boxall standing by a Hawker Audax at Thornaby. The aircraft in the background, Audax serial number K7317, was struck off charge after a forced landing on 19 August 1937.

Group photo of Harley's course at 9 SFTS. Harley is sitting on the front row fifth from the right, while Arthur Scarf is on the front row third from the left. Note the different style of dress between the uniforms worn by the officers and those of the non-commissioned pupils who were destined to become sergeants.

A photo of a Bristol Blenheim at Abingdon being guarded by two policemen during Empire Air Day on 29 May 1937. This particular aircraft, K7051, belonged to 90 Squadron which was based at Bicester. It remained in service until December 1941 when it became an instructional airframe used for training maintenance procedures.

A view of the cockpit and controls of a 62 Squadron Blenheim.

Flying Officer Boxall's Blenheim, L1108, after the incident during a landing at West Fraugh on 14 November 1938.

A group of airmen examining the scene of the accident and damage to the Watch Office at West Fraugh. Note the broken sign stating that 'pilots must report on Arrival and before Departure'.

Norman Irving and on his right Pongo Scarf, both looking very relaxed shortly before their departure for the Far East. Their appearance and white knees suggest that this was one of the first occasions that they had worn Tropical Kit.

A group of airmen preparing to leave for Tengah with Flying Officer Frank Griffiths wearing a crash helmet.

62 Squadron group photo taken at Tengah. Harley is on the back row second from the left, while Pongo Scarf is in the middle row and also second from the left.

Flying Officer Griffiths supervising the loading of supplies while on the ground in Egypt en-route to Singapore.

Harley by one of his favourite cars, a Ford V-8.

Harley standing on the edge of the anchorage at Seletar gazing out across the Johore Straits.

Alor Star even had its own cinema called the 'Empire'.

Harley standing on the left, a half-naked Bertie Keegan in the middle and Pongo Scarf posing in the Pith helmet at Alor Star in 1940.

Sallie Scarf on the left and Harley with his wife Pat, standing outside the hospital at Alor Star.

62 Squadron group photo take at Alor Star. Harley is at the centre of the front row. The back row is made up of a detachment of the Keddah Police who guarded the airfield.

A photo of Harley taken while he was recovering from the 'Desert Island' incident. It is quite noticeable that he still looks pale and weary.

Flight Lieutenant Irving's wedding day with Pongo Scarf standing on the back of a car with what appears to be the lid of a cup on his head. Harley is on the extreme right with a ceremonial sword on his left hip.

Harley meeting the Maharaja of Jodhpur in 1942. The Maharaja is wearing uniform because he held the rank of an Honorary Group Captain in the Indian Air Force.

Harley's wife Pat on the balcony of Baiji Singh's house in Jodhpur, having fun dressing up in Baiji's Saris.

Harley presenting the trophies during Sport's Day at R.A.F. Mauripur in 1943.

Group photo of the staff at 108 Wing in Delhi. Harley is sitting in the front row centre stage.

A more formal photo of Harley in his Number 1 Dress uniform after he had been awarded his medals. Note the Oak Leaf Clasp on the ribbon that represents the 1939-45 War Medal for being Mentioned In Dispatches in January 1945.

An older and more mature looking Harley after his promotion to group captain in 1944.

After being reunited with his family Harley is seen enjoying a picnic with Pat and their daughter Sallie at Maleme Dam in Rhodesia. Situated just outside Bulawayo the dam and its surrounding area was one of Harley's favourite spots.

The Rhodesian Air Force honours Harley and here he is seen being presented with the General Service Medal.

Harley out on the front line while serving as the Commander of a forward airfield during the Bush War.

The name of Arthur Scarf as it appears on the port side of the fuselage of XV109 behind the cockpit windows.

Colonel Paul Edwards, M.B.E., lays a wreath on the grave of Squadron Leader Arthur Scarf, V.C. in December 2008.

RECOMMENDATIONS FOR HONOURS AND AWARDS

Christian Names.. ARTHUR STEWART KING... Surname.... SCARF.......
(in full)   (in block capitals)

Rank.. T/ Squadron Leader .... Official Number... 37693.............

Command or Group.. Far East Command .... Unit........ 62 Squadron,.....

Particulars of meritorious service for which recommendation is made :

On 9th December, 1941, all available Blenheim aircraft of Norgroup, comprising the remnants of Nos. 27 and 62 Squadrons, and a detachment of No. 34 Squadron, assembled at R.A.F. Station Butterworth, were ordered to attack in daylight the advanced operational base of the fighter squadrons of the Japanese Air Force at Singora, Thailand, which were supporting the landing of enemy forces. The aircraft taking part in the sortie were on the point of taking off when a combined dive-bombing and low machine gun attack developed, damaging or destroying all the Blenheims with the exception of one, which had just become airborne a few seconds before the raid started. This aircraft was piloted by Squadron Leader A.S.K. Scarf of No. 62 Squadron, with Sgt. Calder and Sgt. Rich as Navigator/Bomb Aimer and Wireless Operator/Air Gunner respectively.

S/Ldr. Scarf circled the airfield during the attack and witnessed the debacle. When it was over, it would have been entirely reasonable for him to have abandoned the projected operation which was intended to be a formation sortie, but he decided to press home on Singora with his single aircraft. He knew that this individual action could not inflict much material damage but he must have appreciated the moral effect his action would have on the remainder of the Squadron who were helplessly watching their aircraft burning on the ground. Those who knew this officer would realise that he could not have come to any other decision for he was a natural leader, eager to engage the enemy.

He completed his attack successfully in the face of severe opposition, which included attacks by a considerable number of enemy fighters, in the course of which he sustained mortal wounds. The enemy continued to engage him in a running fight which lasted practically to the Malayan border, and his crew testified to the brilliant evasive action he fought in his valiant attempt to return to his base. Owing to his wounds, however, he was unable to do so, but he accomplished a successful forced landing near Alor Star without injury to his crew. Although he was received into hospital, he died shortly after admission.

I suggest that this outstanding act of gallantry and determination in the face of the enemy, and his complete disregard of his personal safety is deserving of the highest award.

State what recognition is recommended. VICTORIA CROSS.(Posthumous)....
State appointment held or how employed.............. Pilot ....
             Recommendation submitted by : G/Capt. N.R. Irving, late 62 Squadron.
             Signature of Commanding Officer.... N.R. IRVING ....

                         Rank............ Group Captain ....

Date.. 18th March, 1946. .... Unit........ Norgroup. ....

Covering remarks of Air Officer Commanding :

        I agree.

             Signature of Air Officer Commanding............
                                              Air Vice Marshal.
Date.. 29.3.46 .... Group. late Far East Command......

Copy of the document submitted by Group Captain Norman Irving recommending that Squadron Leader Arthur Scarf should be awarded the Victoria Cross.

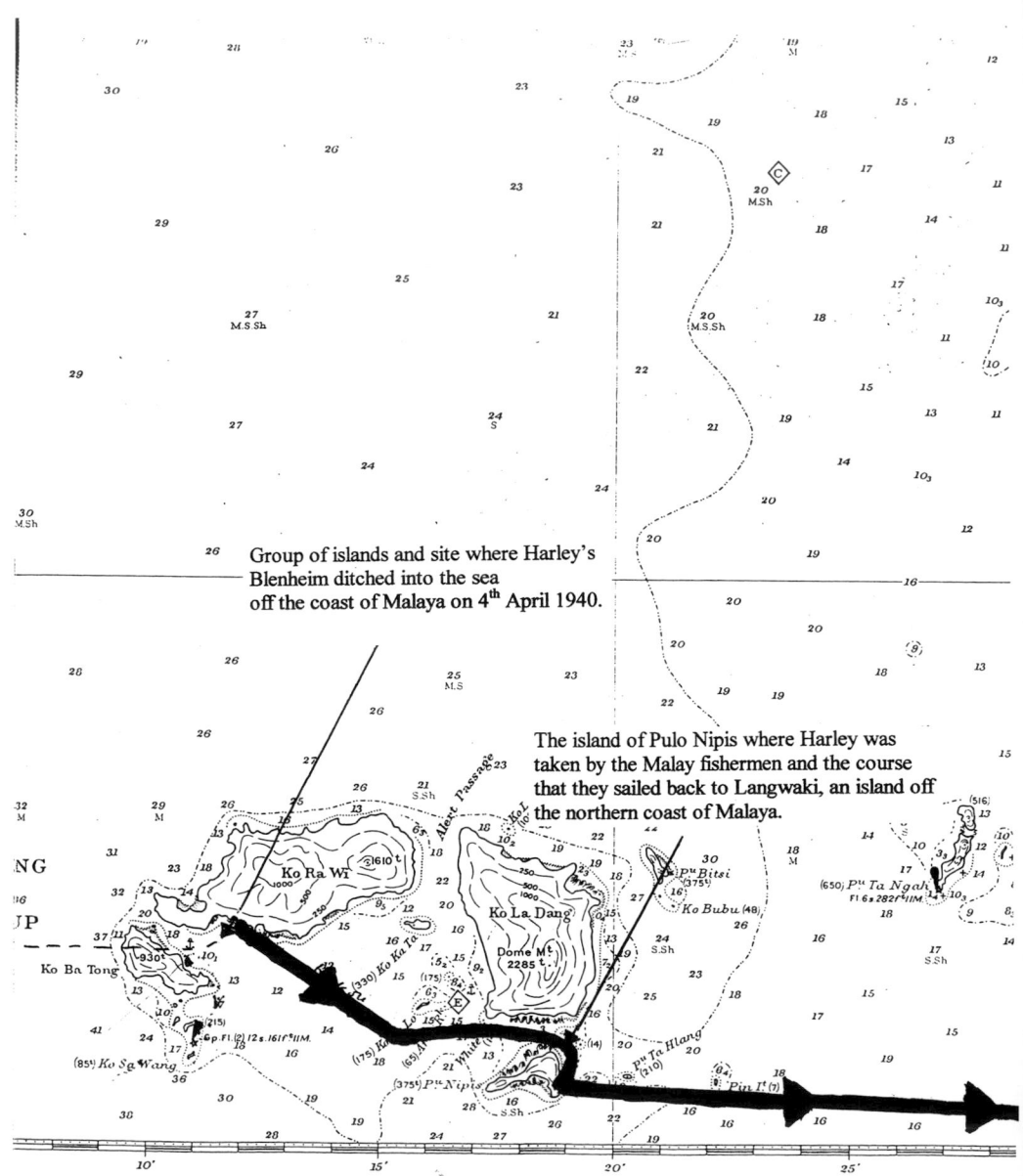

Group of islands and site where Harley's
Blenheim ditched into the sea
off the coast of Malaya on 4th April 1940.

The island of Pulo Nipis where Harley was
taken by the Malay fishermen and the course
that they sailed back to Langwaki, an island off
the northern coast of Malaya.

Map of the group of Butang Islands some forty miles off the coast of Malaya where Harley ditched
his Blenheim in April 1940. The westerly course taken by the Malay fisherman during the voyage
back to Langwaki and the mainland is indicated by the thick black line.

and paying all bills, I said goodbye to Monty and returned by train to Singapore. Apart from the interest of the job it had been a most enjoyable interlude and confirmed my belief that life 'up country' could be much more satisfying than the artificiality of city life in Singapore.

Back at Tengah, I collected the duties of Mess secretary. I was happy to have this job as it kept me occupied out of flying hours and with the new Mess nearing completion, there was plenty of scope for organization.

We were doing a lot of flying these days, mainly long navigational flights in formation and in the afternoon we would fly over to Kallang, the civil airport, for night flying, as our own airfield had not yet been provided with the necessary equipment. Sitting on the balcony of the airport hotel, we would watch the sun sink in the west. Every conceivable colour was reflected in the clouds and, within 15 minutes of the sun touching the horizon, it had slipped beneath the waves. Soon the stars would appear and the radiance of the moon turn night into day. Then, along the twinkling flare path, we would take-off into the placid night air.

In October 62 Squadron took over standby duties and on the 23rd took part in the first exercise that assessed its reaction time and how quickly it could get three aircraft airborne. The signal arrived at 0200 and gave the 'information' that the German ship *Leipzig* was in Singapore waters and ordered that it should be attacked. The squadron had one hour to become airborne from receiving the signal and the Operational Record Book noted that it failed miserably.

On the 26th it was tested again with another simulated threat from a German cruiser called the *Moln* which was, for the purpose of the exercise, said to be off the coast of Singapore. The signal arrived at 0145 and three Blenheims were prepared immediately, but despite the fact that their crews were quick to react, they failed to take-off in the time allotted by Far East HQ. There were problems loading the bombs and it took one hour twelve minutes for them to become airborne from receiving the signal.

At 0345, possibly frustrated by two failed attempts, Far East HQ sent out another signal. Fortunately lessons had been learned from the previous attempts, albeit the hard way. The bombs had already been loaded on to the carriers saving a lot of time, and the three Blenheims were airborne in just 40 minutes.

Kallang was often used by the RAF for night flying and there are several references to the fact that the approaches at Tengah were 'Not Being Clear' and unsuitable for night flying. The former civil airfield at Kallang had a 3,000 feet long grass runway. On Bomber Command airfields in Britain each runway had a cleared area of 100 yards to allow aircraft to overshoot or undershoot in an emergency. In the Far East the nature of the terrain and the limited length of many runways restricted the size of the cleared areas and subsequently safety was affected and training limited.

Off duty, a favourite evening rendezvous, especially if one had a girlfriend, was the Gap which was a road house some five miles out of Singapore, perched on the top of a hill overlooking the harbour. Here, the absolute peacefulness of the place was such that it could almost be felt. Sitting at a small secluded table, lit by a tiny lantern, under the starlit sky, it was conducive to romance. With everyone appearing to talk in whispers and the Chinese 'boys' flitting around noiselessly among the palms, with a cool breeze blowing and soft music in the background, there was no doubt that out here, at least, the best part of the day was the night.

One would never see a Malay at such laborious work; he is far too lazy and feels himself above all manual labour and if he feels the urge to give up squatting in his kampong and come into town, you will find the only domestic job he will undertake will be that of chauffeur – and not a very good one at that. The Malay is nature's gentleman (and perhaps he has the right idea) but it is no wonder that the industrious Chinese monopolizes commercial life and profits from the Malay's indifference to worldly possessions.

The close of the year saw the onset of the north-west monsoon. For three weeks before, the humidity and dry temperatures had been even more uncomfortable. Strong winds and bumpy weather, with towering black cumulus clouds, had made flying less pleasant. At last the tension broke and for twenty-four hours we had a continuous storm, recording over seven inches of rain (one third of the annual rain fall in England). In one hour alone, two-and-a-half inches of rain fell. Storm drains, two to three feet deep, filled to overflowing and, among other things, the underground nest of pythons were flooded causing them to come to the surface en masse to escape drowning.

On 5 November, 62 Squadron received a signal from Far East HQ. It read: 'All aircraft with automatic mixture controls are to be grounded pending an investigation of carburettor trouble.' 62 Squadron was not immediately affected but it was forced to take over standby duties from 34 Squadron until its aircraft and that of other Blenheim units were checked and released back into service.

The following day Pilot Officers Henderson and Fish were detached to Kallang for duties in the operations room. Pilot Officer Frostick was detached to Tengah for similar duties. Their loss caused the strength of 62 Squadron to be reduced to nineteen pilots.

Christmas 1939 was, for most of us, the first occasion at an overseas station, but it was celebrated with the same enthusiasm even if the climate did make it difficult to acquire the festive spirit.

It is the usual custom in service life for the officers to visit the Sergeants' Mess during Christmas morning and, at midday, to serve the airmen with their Christmas dinner. The Airmen's Mess was garlanded for the occasion and the men were in great spirits. They all sat down to dinner together (the only time in the year) and the officers acted as waiters, a gesture of good will handed down by tradition. The meal was good: soup, turkey, with all the trimmings and, of course Christmas pudding. Afterwards, we walked back to our Mess for a cold lunch and slept most of the afternoon in preparation for our Christmas dinner in the evening.

There were about twenty of us dining in; the messing contractor excelled himself and afterwards we made merry. We listened to the King's speech and, when one is many miles from home, it is amazing how near the radio, especially the Empire programme, brings one to one's family in Britain and, in this time of war, how it reminds one that the Empire is knit together as one fighting family in the common cause.

We managed to survive several other parties culminating in a dance at the Tanglin Club on New Year's Eve and I think that most, like myself, were rather glad that Christmas comes only once a year. We were glad to get back into the normal routine. Flying most mornings, my Mess secretarial duties kept me pretty busy in the afternoons as the new Mess was nearing completion and we hoped to move in at the end of January.

Even so most weekends, when not on standby duty, found us yachting in the straits of Jahore. The station now had its own sailing club and possessed several small sailing craft, mainly of native design called 'Kolis' which were small narrow craft with one main sail. The boat was balanced by one of the crew sitting outboard on a plank. They were tricky craft to sail, especially in gusty weather, and many's the ducking we have had when the craft turned turtle in the middle of the straits.

Taffy, the keen sailor with whom I used to sail in the North Sea, had bought himself a thirty foot ocean-going yacht which could sleep four comfortably and in this we used to venture further afield, exploring the numerous small uninhabited islands in these waters. Often, due to the coral outcrop, we would anchor and swim the last hundred yards to the beach, there to eat our sandwiches and fruit before roaming the island.

Though warm, these waters have their disadvantages for swimming as they abound with snakes and jelly fish which can give a nasty sting; the coral near the beach is very sharp and jagged and, in shallow water, one has to pick one's way among foot long sea slugs, harmless though revolting to look at. Sailing became our favourite pastime and its attraction for airmen is not surprising because, as with an aircraft, one uses the elements to further one's ends.

My twenty-seventh birthday occurred in January and, by way of celebration, I took half a dozen of my friends to a Japanese hotel for sukiyaki. We arrived at about 2030 having previously booked our room and were met in the hall with much bowing by an elderly Japanese matron and waiting girls. We were ushered upstairs into a large room devoid of furniture except for a low round table some five feet in diameter with a square hole cut in the centre. Before entering the room we removed our shoes, according to custom, and found it very comfortable walking round on the floor which seemed to be made of many thicknesses of rush matting and quite spongy to the feet.

One of the serving girls brought in a charcoal fire, already lighted and it contained a sort of brazier, which she deposited in the hole in the table. In the meantime we arranged ourselves round the table, sitting cross legged on little straw mats. The girls then proceeded to cook the food which seemed to comprise every conceivable type of meat, fish, onions, chickens' liver and many other ingredients whose origins it was probably better not to enquire. This all ended up in a very tasty stew that we proceeded to eat out of small bowls with the aid of chopsticks. Our first attempts with chopsticks were rather ludicrous but, once having acquired the knack, we became fairly proficient. It was delicious food and we ate our fill, more than I think was good for us as my distended stomach made me feel rather like a Chinese Buddha.

We lay back on the matting in a state of semi-coma and waited for the next item, the Geisha girls. Four little women came into the room in traditional Japanese dress, very correct and solemn. Two of them entered with a peculiar slow shuffle whilst a third sang a song and played a Japanese guitar.

Geisha girls are reputed to be of high caste and are seldom prostitutes. They are supposed to possess all the accomplishments and intelligence necessary to entertain, in the best sense. The two dancing girls were quite attractive in their doll-like fashion and their movements were very languid and rather difficult to understand. The other girl, chanting a sort of dirge and plonking away on her guitar, seemed quite out of tune. Between dances we played some silly sort of table game. It was all very interesting and we left about midnight feeling we had delved a little further into the East and had glimpsed a ritual of an incomprehensible race.

At the end of January we moved into our new Mess. For a week previously most of my time had been spent in final preparations, taking over the inventory, furniture, allocation of quarters, allocation of 'boys' and so on. The Mess was situated on top of a rise overlooking the airfield. The main buildings comprised the dining room and kitchens, anteroom and ladies room, spacious and airy with lofty ceilings. Two blocks of double storied sleeping quarters were built as annexes. Each officer had his own bed-sitting room with hot and cold water laid on, with a passageway leading off from the rear veranda to the ablution block. The front veranda ran the whole length of the block and it was very pleasant to sit out here in the evenings and watch the sun go down below the rubber plantations.

I had my Mess secretary's office in the main building and it was quite a hive of industry, with a Eurasian clerk to keep the books and the Mess corporal assisted by an aircraft hand to run about for me. There were some fifty Chinese 'boys' controlled by No. 1 Boy and generally speaking they made excellent servants.

I had made an acquaintance of the manager of the motor dealers in Singapore and he serviced all the cars belonging to the Sultan of Johore, the native state at the southern tip of the Malay Peninsula adjoining Singapore island. Like so many eastern potentates he had a stable of fine motor vehicles, amongst which was a colossal supercharged Mercedes, previously owned by Earl Howe. My friend arranged for me to drive this car and one day I took it out on the main road which crosses the island, a fine wide stretch of concrete, and pushed it to 120 mph. The power was terrific, especially when one pushed open the last inch of the throttle which brought in the supercharger.

Arrangements had been made for me to drive this car in a speed hill climb which was to take place shortly but, at the last moment, to my great disappointment, the Sultan decided to withdraw as he thought that his entry might be frowned upon, the car being of German origin. Nevertheless it had been a great thrill driving this car, even though it did only seven miles to the gallon.

Falling from the sublime to the ridiculous, I purchased an old Hillman Straight '8' Tourer for the sum of $150 (£24) which proved to be an economical proposition as the taxi fare into Singapore was $2 per trip. Having passed a driving test and obtained the necessary licence, I experienced for the first time the hazards of driving in this part of the world. In the city and villages, natives and animals wander all over the roads and, in Singapore itself, one has to literally clear a way amongst the hundreds of old bicycles and rickshaws, at the same time maintaining a sharp lookout for native driven taxis and trucks. Hand signals to them, it appeared, were just a waste of time and the general method of driving was in top gear with the accelerator hard down on the floorboards.

We were doing a lot of flying these days. It was particularly pleasant at night and in the early morning when the air was cool and as calm as a millpond. Later in the day when the sun had risen in the heavens, the air became more turbulent and in the afternoon very bumpy and we landed with shirts and shorts saturated with perspiration.

At the end of March, as a very welcome break from the artificial life in Singapore, my flight was ordered to Alor Star. News had been received that German merchantmen were in the harbour of Sabang, the most north-easterly tip of Sumatra, Dutch East Indies and they were expected to make a dash for their homeland. By this time our Blenheims were getting a bit antiquated. We had had them for two years and spares were not always readily available as, obviously, the squadrons fighting in Europe had top priority. We badly needed replacement engines, and our range was literally limited by our oil consumption.

However, our five aircraft flew north the 400 miles and landed at Alor Star, the most north-westerly landing ground in Malaya, thirty miles from the border with Siam. This was the same airfield at which we had landed six months earlier on our way through to Singapore, and we were delighted to be back. A hangar and flight offices were readily available but domestic accommodation had not yet been built, so that twenty of us, aircrews and ground crews, lived in a rest house at Kepala Batas, on the other side of the airfield. This was run by an enormous Chinese, and he looked after us very well; with a purpose no doubt as, soon after the Japanese invasion, he was arrested and shot as an enemy spy.

CHAPTER 7

Lost at Sea

We were in constant radio communication with air headquarters and at all times two aircraft and crews were on 'readiness'. On Thursday 4 April I was in the flight office with my crew on standby duty when a signal came through from air headquarters that two aircraft were to make a reconnaissance of Sabang harbour and photograph any shipping therein. We roused the other crew, prepared our flight plan and went out to our aircraft which were already started up.

The five Blenheims were under the command of Squadron Leader L.V. Spencer, the 'B' flight commander. Flying Officer Boxall and his two crew consisting of Sergeant Rodger, the navigator, and LAC Martin, wireless operator, took-off from Alor Star at 1030.

I was elated to be the pilot of the first operational flight of our squadron during the war. We were airborne at 1030 and set course almost due west for the 350-mile crossing of the Straits of Malacca, with my support aircraft formating on my starboard quarter. The crossing was uneventful and Sabang harbour appeared through the haze after 1 hour 45 minutes flying. We had been instructed to keep wireless silence during this operation but I was in contact by radio telephony with the other aircraft and, forming line astern, we roared down to a few hundred feet over Sabang.

The harbour was surrounded on three sides by high cliffs but, by dint of manoeuvring and steep turns within the basin, the air gunner in the rear cockpit was able to get some good shots. Two merchant ships lay alongside the wharf and, although we could not identify them by any national markings, they were undoubtedly the enemy craft we sought. As Holland was still a neutral country, not yet having been invaded, we could not attack them in this harbour but had to wait for them to come out into open waters.

Also moored in the harbour was a Dutch flying boat and, after we had been flying around for some time, we saw that it had started its engines and was taxiing across the harbour for take-off. We did not wish to create an international incident with this supposedly neutral flying boat as we were well inside Dutch territorial waters and so, having exhausted our supply of film and feeling that we had accomplished our mission, we turned and headed for the open sea.

I called up the pilot of the other aircraft on the radio telephony to resume our formation preparatory to returning to base, but I got no reply and, as he was nowhere in sight, I assumed that he had already set course for Alor Star independently, although this was against orders and, as it transpired, was an unfortunate action to have taken. I found out a week or so later that my surmise was correct and that he landed safely.

Leaving Sabang behind at 1300, I put the aircraft into a climb to gain height for the long return sea crossing. I had gained an altitude of 9,000 feet when, some forty miles from the coast of Sumatra, the oil pressure of my starboard engine fell to zero. I levelled off the aircraft and throttled back on this engine, opened up the port engine and, with a reduced airspeed of 110 mph (compared with the normal cruising of 170 mph), trimmed the aircraft to fly on one engine. I now had to decide whether to return and make a forced landing in Sumatra with consequent internment, or to attempt the odd 300 miles across the sea on one engine. It was an unenviable decision to make as I had the lives of my crew to consider, but there was really no choice so I decided to keep going – anyway, we had some jolly good photos to deliver and there was a reasonable chance that the port engine would carry us home.

My navigator, Sergeant Rodger, sitting alongside me was, of course, fully aware of what was going on but rightly or wrongly, I did not tell my wireless operator, Leading Aircraftman Martin, crouched over his radio, keeping wireless watch for any signals that might come in. As I have said, our orders were not to transmit any messages and I did not consider that the present emergency warranted breaking this wireless silence. And LAC Martin, being such a youngster, I thought would be happier in sublime ignorance of our predicament.

The propeller of the dead engine continued to rotate slowly but after ten minutes the reduction gear seized and it twisted itself off its shaft and disappeared into the ocean below. This was not a bad thing in itself, as it reduced the drag and gave us a slightly increased speed.

After a while the port engine, labouring under the increased strain, started to overheat and I reduced the revolutions to give us an airspeed of 95 mph. This was not much above stalling point and the aircraft felt very soggy although it managed to maintain height at 9,000 feet. But with the trimming tabs fully extended I could not keep her straight and my left leg ached due to the constant pressure I had to exert on the rudder bar. I could only keep level by holding up the starboard wing with the aileron control.

We limped along like this for nearly 90 minutes when an island appeared through the haze beneath. At this particular moment, the oil pressure on the port engine started to fluctuate and I was in two minds whether to keep on going or to force land on this island. In this case, fortunately, my mind was made up for me as, within a minute or so, the port engine seized and we were flying in silence. I reset the trimming tabs, turned off the petrol supply and put the aircraft into a gentle glide.

Being at 9,000 feet, it would take us a good five minutes before we hit the water. I told Martin to send out an SOS and give our position which Rodger was working out from his chart. As we glided down through the haze, in peaceful silence without the roar of the engines, it became clear that the island we had seen was, in fact, a group of islands but, by this time, we were near the water and all my attention was concentrated on making a decent landing. I manoeuvred the aircraft so that we should land on the sea 250-300 yards from the shore heading towards a narrow beach. I ordered Rodger to take up his assigned ditching position aft with the wireless operator.

Now we were almost on top of the water and I eased back on the control column. Holding off as long as possible, I felt the tail of the aircraft cleave the waves and I hauled hard back on the stick, feeling the crippled craft sink slowly deeper into the sea. I think it would have been a good ditching and that we might have skated up the beach and got out with dry feet but, within a few seconds ploughing through the water at about 70 mph, we were suddenly impaled on an outcrop of coral just beneath the surface and stopped dead. Although my safety belt was fastened tight, I was thrown violently forward on to the dashboard, momentarily stunned but immediately revived by a wave of water pouring in through the opened hatch above my head.

The first indication that the aircraft had been lost occurred when Flying Officer Frank Griffiths was handed a W/T message shortly after reporting for duty in the operations room at Alor Star. It stated that Harley's aircraft had ditched into the sea close to an island called Pulo Perak. He always maintained that a Sunderland flying boat from 230 Squadron was airborne within twenty minutes of him receiving the message.

I clambered out along the wing of the stricken aircraft, grabbed the dinghy pack from the two in the gunner's cockpit and threw it into the sea where it opened and inflated. Rodger and Martin climbed through the gunner's hatch and piled into the dinghy, where I joined them, tossed about in a heavy swell. Unfortunately, the string which was attached to the fuselage of the aircraft from the valve in the dinghy would not break as it should have done and the heavy swell threatened to turn the aircraft, pivoted on the coral, onto its back at any moment with the incipient danger of dragging the dinghy to the bottom. So I climbed back into the aircraft, now completely flooded, and with my head under water located the knot and untied it – it seemed to take hours.

Now freed from the sinking aircraft, we paddled for the shore but we soon found that the tide race was carrying us out to sea. Rodger could not swim, so Martin and I went over the side and swam 200 yards to the beach pulling the dinghy behind us. The last few yards we waded through the coral, heedless of the cuts inflicted, and fell exhausted on the beach. We silently thanked God for our deliverance. Having recovered our breath we stripped off our sodden clothing and took stock of the situation. We felt ourselves extremely lucky to have got off so lightly. Apart from the cuts inflicted by coral, our only injuries were bumps and bruises, although Martin had a couple of deep gashes in one shinbone. It was most fortunate that none of us had suffered any broken bones. I suppose we were all shocked to a certain extent, but our feelings were of great elation at our escape and we thought it would only be a matter of hours before a ship or flying boat would appear to restore us to civilization.

It was now 1500 and nothing had passed our lips for eight hours. We were hungry and parched and our first thought was to find some water fit to drink. Our emergency rations had gone to the bottom of the ocean when the belly of the aircraft had been ripped out by the coral reef and, even if they had been salvageable, we did not feel like going back into the turbulent sea. The aircraft by this time, disintegrating under the continual sawing motion on the jagged reef, had now almost disappeared beneath the waves.

The island we had landed on proved (on later exploration) to be roughly two miles long by one mile across, rising steeply from the shore to a height of about 400 feet and covered with thick jungle down to the water's edge. The coastline was made up of small sandy beaches 100-200 yards long, bounded by huge boulders and mangrove. At high water the sea came to within twenty feet of the jungle.

We probed into the undergrowth in search of water and found a brackish pond which quenched our raging thirst. This pool was at the top of the very beach on which we had landed and it is remarkable to record that, in all our subsequent explorations, we found no other water fit to drink. We searched for food but found only one tree bearing a very sour fruit. But we were not really bothered about this as it would only be a matter of hours before we would be picked up.

It was getting late in the afternoon and it seemed more likely that our rescue would not be effected until the following day, so we set about collecting wood to build a fire. Fortunately, our matches had dried in the hot sun, but we were not able to smoke our water-damaged cigarettes. Soon we had a blazing fire going and built up a stack of wood to keep it replenished during the night, partly for warmth but mainly as a beacon to guide our rescuers.

We were uncertain of the nature of the animal life on the island so we thought it would be advisable to sleep in the dinghy moored to a pole which was standing out of the water some thirty feet from the shore. And as darkness fell, we paddled out and tied up to this stake. As a precautionary measure against drifting away, I tied another piece of string from the pole to my wrist.

We were all feeling rather weary and settled ourselves down to sleep. But we soon discovered that the dinghy had sprung a leak – it had probably got torn on the coral – so we waded back to the beach and slept around the fire. We took it in turns to keep watch throughout the night – one hour on watch, two hours' sleep.

My companions slept fitfully on the hard sand. The blazing fire threw strange shadows into the jungle, now awakened for its nocturnal cacophony, the shrillness of the millions of insects providing a deafening background to the strange squawks and grunts of unseen animals. Occasionally the light of the fire would be reflected in a pair of burning eyes peering out of the undergrowth, which then quickly disappeared. The soothing wash of the waves, now quieted after the turmoil of the day, lapped gently on the shore, and I felt at peace with the world.

Despite the loss of Harley and his crew, there was an urgent need for intelligence about the whereabouts of the German merchantmen, that necessitated another reconnaissance sortie should be flown on this day. The operation was carried out by Squadron Leader Spencer and his crew composed of Sergeants Warwick and Bury. They took-off from Alor Star in Blenheim L1234 at 0720 and returned safely after a sortie that lasted 3 hours 55 minutes.

The search for Harley's aircraft continued but as it was being conducted approximately fifty-five miles away from their actual position, it was hardly surprising that nothing was found. Pulo Rawi (Ko Ra Wi) was situated eighty miles off the western coast of Malaya and it was one of a group off such islands. Although Harley did not realize it at the time, it was part of the territory of Siam, a pro-Axis country and they were at risk of being interned, or worse.

Day Two – Friday 5 April

The welcome dawn brought warmth to our chilled bodies and we set about collecting more fuel for the fire to build it up to aid our rescuers who must surely be close at hand. We searched for anything in the way of food but it was incredible how, with profuse vegetation abounding, there was nothing fit for human consumption.

This was in the days when the art of survival on the sea and in the jungle had not received much attention. Later it was to become a specialist study, all aircrews carried their own survival kits and dinghies were elaborately fitted out with rations and water, fishing lines and so on. I suppose, in a small way, the experience we were undergoing assisted in the development in these aids to survival. As it was, we had nothing except the dinghy, two distress rockets, a two gallon tin and the rotting clothes we stood up in. There were no fish in the shallow waters and we had not even a bent pin to try our luck in the sea.

We wrote SOS in ten feet high letters in the sand, with leaves and twigs, and sat in the shade of the mangrove to escape the blistering sun, awaiting our rescuers. In the afternoon, two ships appeared on the horizon – warships apparently, judging by their wide superstructure. We made smoke signals with wet leaves and at dusk built up the fire into a huge blaze. After dark we fired one of our distress rockets; the other one was wet and just fizzled like a damp squib. We thought they must have seen our signals and would pick us up in the morning.

Discussing the trend of events that evening we thought it rather strange that no aircraft had appeared during the day as we knew that the immediate action to our

SOS signal, which had been acknowledged by the W/T station at Alor Star, would have been to send out aircraft to search for us. And the doubt came into our minds that the island we were on was not the one we had given in our emergency signal.

Our charts had been lost in the crash landing, but Rodger recalled that the name of the island he had passed to Martin for transmission was Pulo Perak. This is a small isolated island jutting out of the sea between Sumatra and Malaya, a hundred miles from the nearest land; an impossible place to land. We had often flown to this pinpoint in the sea on navigational exercises and I remembered it quite distinctly. This island we were on, one of a group, was obviously not Pulo Perak, and the sombre truth became only too clear that the search which was undoubtedly being carried out in the Pulo Perak area would report no trace and we should be give up for lost.

Our otherwise cheerful spirits were somewhat dampened as the true import of our deduction sank in. One could not blame Rodger for misreading our position on the chart as it had been difficult to keep the yawing aircraft true on course and, in the excitement of the last few minutes, coming down through the haze, he naturally thought that the island for which we were heading was Pulo Perak which was almost on our track. In any case, as captain of the aircraft, the responsibility was mine and, in normal circumstances, I would have checked his position. We found out later that the island we were on, Pulo Rawi, was actually sixty miles north by east of Pulo Perak. It was, therefore, not to be wondered that, having given our position as Pulo Perak, the search in progress did not extend as far as the group of islands in which we had force landed.

We knew that, by this time, casualty signals would have been sent off to our next-of-kin reporting us missing and we were disturbed at the unnecessary grief and anxiety that this news would cause to our loved ones when all the time we were safe and well. Our main hope was that we should be rescued within the next few days before the final fatal signals 'missing believed killed' would be dispatched. Nevertheless our spirits were high and we laughed and joked the evening away. We built up our fire and turned in, continuing our watches throughout the night.

The realization that they were not where they thought they were must have been a frightening prospect and Sergeant Rodger may have felt very guilty about making such a mistake. Their worst fears had already been realized and Harley's father received the telegram from the Air Ministry on this day.

For the families of all three airmen it must have been a shock to receive such bad news but Harley's family had already had more than their share of it in the past. Harley's father, John Elliott Boxall, who was a joiner, had already lost his wife and eldest son in quite tragic circumstances. In 1924 Harley's brother Robert, who was only 14 year old, had died of diphtheria after catching an infection while attending a scout camp.

In 1933 Harley's mother, Emma, was hit by a horse and buggy and was badly injured as she crossed the street in Walsall. The injury was so bad that she had to have her leg amputated and she died soon afterwards of septicaemia. Mr Boxall later remarried the housekeeper, with whom Harley got on very well and he always referred to her as Mater.

Harley's father had never been keen on him joining the RAF in the first place and so one can only imagine the thoughts that went through his mind when he received the telegram. There would have been few details in the telegram to explain what had happened but within a few days the CO of 62 Squadron, Wing Commander Farnhill, would write to all three families giving them more information.

Day Three – Saturday 6 April

The third day dawned bringing with it renewed hope. We had now been forty-eight hours without food and felt the pangs of hunger. We wandered along the beach and collected more wood and each ate one of those unripe 'plums'. But they were extremely sour and the consequences were painful. We tried several types of leaves but they were bitter and unappetizing.

Our local explorations had convinced us that the island was uninhabited but there were signs that it had been lived on. From the remains of an atap hut and the stake in the water, it appeared that it might have been used by the Malays as an occasional fishing ground. This was a comforting thought, the main conjecture being when next it would be visited.

About midday our spirits soared as across the bay, some three miles distant, a small coastal steamer came into view and anchored off an island separated from us by a channel about a mile-and-a-half across. We threw dried leaves onto the fire and soon clouds of smoke were billowing up. We tried to relight our second rocket but it was still too wet to ignite. We hurried along the beach to get to the point nearest to the steamer, clambering over the rocks along the coastline for about a mile, saturated with spray and swimming round the rocky promontories, heedless of the cuts inflicted by the coral. At last we reached the point where we were directly opposite the steamer. We waved our shirts and shouted, tried to light another fire on the spot but the wind was too strong for our few remaining matches. There was no sign of recognition from the ship although we could vaguely discern the movement of human beings on board.

Martin said he would go on to reach narrower waters and swim across the channel. I forbade him to do this as the strong tidal race running between the islands would have made an attempt most hazardous. He went on, I caught him and expressly ordered him not to go, but he slipped from my grasp and disappeared round the promontory. After an interminable time, weakened by shouting but with eyes glued to the steamer, we perceived more smoke coming from the funnel and it slowly pulled away from its anchorage. It was turning in a wide arc and coming straight towards us. Here at last was our salvation. We leapt madly upon the rocks and waved and shouted until we were hoarse.

But the turning circle of the steamer continued – we were frantic in our excitement – and it pulled away, not noticing us, and disappeared away from sight amongst the islands. Our spirits just about touched rock bottom, but my main concern was what had happened to Martin. We waited for a time and then, leaving Rodger, I went on to look for him. Across the narrow beaches, crawling around the rocky promontories, I went on to a point beyond which I felt he would not have gone, but there was no sign of him. I wandered slowly back greatly distressed with the thought that he had undoubtedly perished in his gallant attempt to swim across the channel.

I found Rodger sitting disconsolately on the beach. There was no need for me to tell him that I had not found Martin, he must have read it in my face. I decided that we ought to return to our base as there was no point in waiting. With the tide rising, we should be hard pressed to get back before darkness fell, and we had to return as our only supply of drinking water was on that beach. Before we left, we wrote in large letters in the sand: 'Martin – return to camp' It was all we could do.

The sun had set by the time we got back, but the embers of the fire rekindled our spirits. We assuaged our thirst with the brackish water and collected sufficient wood to keep the fire going during the night.

We had been resting for about an hour when out of the shadows a form appeared and, heaven be praised, Martin staggered in. His return cleared the despondency from our hearts and we were overjoyed at being together again. Poor fellow, he was almost all in, but when he had rested for a while he told us that he had attempted to cross the narrows but that the tide had been too strong for him and it was all he could do to regain the beach. It was a very gallant attempt.

We were all too tired to keep any watch that night so we slept where we lay, each replenishing the fire as he woke from fitful sleep during the night. It was very cold with a heavy dew and we huddled together, unsheltered from the elements.

According to what was reported later by 62 Squadron's Commanding Officer, the search was abandoned during the evening of the 6th. Despite some reports from the press to suggest that it went on for several more days, it seems quite unlikely that it did. It is just possible that the steam ship that they saw was a supply ship that was taking part in the search and Martin's instincts may have been correct!

Day Four – Sunday 7 April

We awoke at dawn on this fourth day, feeling cold and stiff, with dampness still in our bones. It was now seventy-two hours since we had eaten. The hunger pains in our stomachs had receded but we were now beginning to feel physically weak. The brackish water kept us alive. During the heat of the day, we would several times lay in the shallow waters as a relief from the hard sand, absorbing the life-sustaining salt into our bodies.

We collected more dry wood for our fire, but each day we had to go further afield which taxed our diminishing strength. The various leaves we sampled were revoltingly inedible. During one of our excursions we found an old enamel mug and, prising off the rock what looked like winkles, we boiled these minute shell fish over the fire The difficulty was to get at the meat, but Rodger happened to have a nail file in his pocket which we used, in turn, to prise out the morsel. It was a long job but at least we were eating.

Hauling wood and searching the rocks was tiring work. Our feet had swollen so that we could not wear our shoes and the cuts in our feet picked up the blistering sand. During the heat of the day we lay beneath the trees, but we got little rest from the millions of ants and the swarms of flies, like bluebottles, which bit into our flesh and drew blood.

In spite of these hardships, we kept remarkably cheerful, young Martin's high spirits setting a perfect example. We were now beginning to look thoroughly disreputable with the real ship-wrecked mariner touch. Our khaki drill uniform hung in rags and beards began to sprout; Rodger's coming on very nicely being a dark haired man.

I was beginning to feel a little worried about Rodger. He did not seem to have got over the disappointment of the coastal steamer episode and would sit for hours without saying a word, or wander off alone along the beach. We did what we could to cheer him up, but it was obvious that he was beginning to feel the strain. We had begun to build a beacon of dried wood and leaves, to be lit when necessary and whilst it was essential to conserve one's strength as far as possible, Rodger would attack this task with such ferocity of purpose that within a short time he would become exhausted, leaving him more morose than before.

At low tide, we set out along the beach further afield than we had been before when, rounding a promontory, we saw a village in the distance with washing out to dry. We hurried towards it, our flagging spirits revived, but the hallucination turned out to be a group of rocks and the 'washing' was the white sand gleaming behind the mangrove. We arrived back in camp in the late afternoon. We scraped the paint off one side of our petrol tin and tried to polish it with sand for use as a heliograph, but without much success. Soon the sun dropped below the horizon and the chill night air enveloped us. We huddled together by the fire and fell into an uneasy sleep.

Day Five – Monday 8 April

The warm sun at dawn awoke us on the fifth morning, seeping into our bones and bringing new hope for the day. But there was no doubt that our strength was greatly reduced and it was as much as we could do to collect wood for the fire. Again smoke appeared on the horizon and we tried our heliograph, but it came no nearer. Rodger persevered with the beacon which was now about eight feet high, while Martin and I penetrated into the jungle on another search for food.

It was very hard going and after an hour we had made only 300 yards headway. It was infuriating that, with all the hum of nature about us, there was nothing to be found which was edible. We occasionally saw a large iguana dart back into the undergrowth and we could hear the chattering of monkeys high in the trees; a glorious tropical bird would flit across in the branches above, but all were out of our grasp.

Back on the beach, a few tiny land crabs came up for air and we pounced on these and put them in our mug to boil; we chewed them, spitting out the gritty bits. Perhaps our ears were deceiving us but we thought we heard an aircraft behind us, on the other side of the island, but it never appeared.

In the afternoon there was a particularly low tide and the tail of the aircraft appeared above the surface of the gentle swell. Martin and I waded out through the coral outcrop and clambered on board. We salvaged a Lewis gun and two pans of ammunition – 200 rounds – as we thought it might come in useful as a sound signal, also a fabric engine cover that we dried in the sun and used as a blanket.

The swift setting of the sun brought to a close another day. Rodger was now obviously feeling the strain and without Martin's cheerfulness I fear he might have become unbalanced. The lack of food drained our reserves of strength considerably and our bones showed up through the taut skin. I know I found it impossible to assume a normal sitting position as the bottom of my spine touched the hard ground. I realized that our situation was becoming serious, but we were helpless to do anything about it. We could, no doubt, survive many more days sustained by our brackish water supply, but the sooner we were rescued the better, particularly for Rodger's sake, before our overtaxed hearts and bodies suffered any permanent impairment.

Even in these near-desperate circumstances, I somehow felt all along that we were not destined to rot on this island and that help would reach us before it was too late. Pulling the engine cover over us, grateful for its protection from the damp night air, we drifted into the realms of unconsciousness.

Day Six – Tuesday 9 April

It rained heavily during the night and we welcomed the rising of the sun on this sixth morning, absorbing its warmth into our aching bodies. We went about our daily tasks of collecting wood, but it was a slow process as any effort brought on palpitations and the weakness of our limbs necessitated frequent rest. We lay in the shade of the jungle and stripped the Lewis gun, cleaned it as best as we could after its five days immersion in seawater and then reassembled it.

We had fitted a round into the breach to fire a bullet through the barrel when a boat came silently round the edge of the mangrove, heading for our beach. We were spellbound, and looked again; yes, it was a boat, a small native fishing boat with human beings on board. Rodger snatched up the Lewis gun, but I took it from him and threw it into the undergrowth. We didn't speak; we didn't want to frighten them away.

Stepping out onto the beach, we walked slowly towards the boat, waving timidly. And then, gaining courage as the vessel still continued in our direction, we broke into a trot, strange noises came from our throats and we dashed into the water and hauled the boat up to the shore.

The Malay fishermen were as astonished to see us as we were thankful to see them. They could not understand these strange wild-looking white men shaking them by the hand and hugging them, laughing hysterically and dragging them up the beach.

When the first excitement of our deliverance had subsided, we endeavoured to explain to the fishermen how we came to be there. But it was difficult to make them understand in our few words of Malay. I remembered the word for aeroplane – 'Kepal terbang', ship of the air – but even this did not convey much to them, their way of living being so primitive. Fortunately, Rodger had a RAF diary with him in which a photograph of an aircraft was still fairly discernable despite frequent immersion in salty water and this, together with much sign language depicting our crash, and pointing out the stern of our aircraft still visible above the waves, eventually made clear to them our presence on this island. Gradually they began to understand and there was much consternation amongst them – a wizened old man of about eighty years, his son of about sixty and three young boys. We let them get over their surprise then I said, 'Mau machan – tida macham' (six) hari', meaning 'Want food – no food for six days'. Without delay the old man spoke to the boys who went back to the boat and fetched a large cauldron of rice that they placed on our fire to heat up. Then they produced a basket of what looked like ping-pong balls but which we learned were turtles' eggs; these they put on to boil in a separate vessel of water. We continued to converse as far as possible but we could hardly wait until the meal was cooked. The smell of warm rice tickled our nostrils and permeated to our empty stomachs.

In the meantime, they had brought up several green coconuts from the boat and with a deft slash of a hatchet cut away an outer portion so that we could drink the delicious milk, ice-cold and tasting like nectar. Soon the meal was cooked and, producing small bowls, the old man served us with rice and showed us how to nip the soft shells of the turtle's egg to get at the yoke which was a hard yellow ball.

We ate until our shrunken stomachs were distended, washed down with the delicious coconut milk. Without any doubt the best meal we had ever had in our lives. Then the old man produced some native cigarettes, reeds about six inches in length packed with tobacco. We gratefully accepted his offer to smoke, but the strong tobacco in our weakened condition set our heads reeling.

During our difficult conversation, I had been endeavouring to find out where we were and to make the old gentleman understand that we wanted to be taken back to Alor Star, Kedah. I gathered that we were on an island called Pulo Rawi but, without our charts, this did not mean very much and to the fisherman, the name Alor Star or Kedah did not mean much either. I handed him a Malayan $5 note to signify our intention of rewarding him, but he just turned it over in his hands and passed it over to his son for inspection. It did not mean anything to either of them, obviously they had never seen paper money before.

The old man kept his eye on the sun and, towards midday, indicated that we should leave. We were only too glad to get away from this island which had so nearly become our grave and, feeling fortified in strength and spirit, we helped them carry their utensils to the boat and climbed on board.

The boat was only about 20 feet in length, similar to the Kolis we had sailed round Singapore, and with eight of us on board it was down to the gunwales. The single sail was raised and the balancing board pushed to one side, along which one of the young boys scooted out with the agility of a monkey. Fortunately, the sea was calm and the breeze, filling the sail, carried us away from the inhospitable island of Rawi.

We sailed through the group of islands (the Butang Group) and, at sunset, approached another island, the most easterly in the group, called Pulo Nipis, where there was a fishing village above the shore. All the inhabitants, about 100 all told, came out to see what strange creatures the old fisherman had brought back with him. A most primitive type of people, they eyed us with interest and we were not quite sure whether we should be murdered on the spot or put in a pot to boil. They led us to a hut raised on piles above the ground, the old man explaining his catch to the villagers as we went along. There was much murmuring amongst them but we felt a certain amount of re-assurance when they produced food; rice, dried fish and more of the deliciously fresh coconut milk. I remember remarking to Martin to keep his eye off the women. As darkness fell, a ferocious looking individual came into the hut and lit an oil-burning lamp; but they left us to ourselves and, settling down on the rush covered floor, we were soon asleep.

On this day it was reported by the British Press that the air search had been called off and it seemed there was little hope that the three airmen would be found. Mr Boxall received the news by telegram. It was also the day that Wing Commander Farnhill wrote to the families and there was little comfort to be gained from his carefully chosen words:

Dear Mr Boxall,

May I express my deepest sympathy which I, in common with all officers and men of the squadron, feel for you in your sorrow and the loss of your son in a flying accident. I am afraid that although he is still posted as 'Missing – Believed Killed', it is impossible to hold out any further hope that he is still alive.

In the circumstances I am unable to give you any definite details of the cause of the accident and all I know is that your son took-off to carry out a reconnaissance on the morning of 4th April and that he was returning after completing his task, having been in signal communication with his base all the time, when he sent an S.O.S. message saying that he was about to make a forced landing. Two flying boats were sent out immediately which arrived at the position indicated 1 hour and 18 minutes later after the last signal had been received. They were, however, unable to discover any track of the aircraft or crew on the island and although the search continued all that day and up to the evening of the 6th April, with all available aircraft and a supply ship, no trace has been found on any islands in the vicinity or in the sea within a radius of fifty miles of the position indicated and it must now be presumed that the aircraft and crew are lost. The aircraft was equipped with a collapsible dinghy and the crew with life jackets, so something must have happened suddenly at the end which made the aircraft crash instead of carrying out a forced landing, and all the crew must have been killed instantly. This is pure surmise, for otherwise some members of the crew would have been able to make use of the life saving arrangements and must have been found.

I am afraid that is all we shall ever know of the accident, as although the aircraft was in communication with its base during the whole reconnaissance, no indication of any trouble was given until the forced landing signal. A Court of Inquiry has, however, been convened, and if I can tell you anything further about the accident, I will do so in due course.

It is difficult to soften a blow of this sort and we all feel it as a great personal loss. I have known Harley as his Flight Commander and Commanding Officer since 1938, and I have always had the highest admiration for him. His work was an example to all ranks and never failing cheerfulness at all times have been a great help in the squadron. He has been recommended for employment on the Staff which is a rare tribute to an officer of his length of service. The work on which your son was engaged at the time of the accident was essential and just as much a factor in the prosecution of the war as if he had been flying over Germany.

A Committee of Adjustment has been formed to deal with your son's affairs in this country, but they are unable to communicate with you until instructions have been received from the Air Ministry to proceed. In the meantime all his effects are being kept in safe custody.

Again I assure you of my deepest sympathy.

Yours sincerely,

G. Farnhill. Wing Commander

Day Seven – Wednesday 10 April

We woke up with a start when a tom-tom suddenly started booming; but after a few minute it ceased and, waiting in silence for some time, we returned to an uneasy sleep. The soft light of dawn filtered through the bamboo walls of our hut, and we took stock of our surroundings. The single room was about ten feet square by six feet high and was completely unfurnished, except for a framed print of some gentleman in what appeared to be an admiral's uniform, highly coloured in the eastern style, which hung on one of the walls.

We tried to decipher certain hieroglyphics which surrounded the portrait, but they were certainly not in Malay script. An emblem surmounted the picture and it dawned on us that it must be the badge of Siam. If this meant we were on a Siamese island, our troubles were not yet over as Siam was a neutral country and we were in imminent danger of being interned.

Our cogitations were interrupted by the door being pushed open and a native entered bringing a tray of rice and dried fish and three vessels of weak tea. We made a hearty breakfast of this meal, meanwhile discussing the immediate problem. Having got so far, we certainly had no intention of being interned in Siam if a possible alternative presented itself.

Shortly afterwards, about twenty ferocious looking Malays crowded into the room and squatted down, filling the room to overflowing. I opened the conversation by trying to convey to them our thanks for their hospitality, food and shelter, although most of my vocabulary consisted of the words 'Terima kasi' meaning 'Thank you', with suitable signs and actions. Not one of them could understand English. Then I tried to convey to them that we would like them to take us to Alor Star, but I gleaned from their murmurings amongst themselves and their facial expressions that they were not keen on the idea. I persevered on this line, a few more Malay words coming into my head and told them that they would be paid for their services.

I mentioned a sum of $60 – why $60 I cannot remember as this was equivalent to only £7 sterling, a very cheap ransom for the return of three fully trained aircrew. However it seemed a lot of money to them, and at least we had reached some basis for discussion. I could not get over their reluctance to take us to the mainland; and then it occurred to me that, if we were in fact on a Siamese island, they would probably be diffident to land on foreign territory. They kept mentioning the name 'Pulo Taratau' – another island but this name meant absolutely nothing to us.

I tried to visualize the map and came to the conclusion that we were probably north of the international boundary and Taratau was another island laying between our present haven and the mainland; and, not recognizing the name, was also more likely to be Siamese territory. We must avoid being taken there at all costs as there we would, without doubt, run into Siamese officialdom, which was more pro-Japanese than pro-British, with almost certain internment to follow.

Concentrating on the map in my mind, I remembered that Langkawi, a large island settlement some thirty miles from Alor Star was just south of the international boundary – in fact, the international boundary ran between Taratau and Langkawi, separated by a channel some forty-five miles across – and so I decided to switch my argument in favour of being taken to Langkawi which was definitely part of British Malaya and would not necessitate such a long sea voyage for our rescuers. I brought the name Langkawi into the conversation and it was immediately apparent that the island was known to them. At last we were getting somewhere; but still they were reluctant to come to an agreement, and persisted in their suggestion to take us to this place named Taratau.

The argument went on throughout the morning. The atmosphere of the hut became stifling with so many beings crammed into the confined space but, although my body was wilting, I was determined to overcome this last obstacle to freedom. I concentrated on the Ringit they would receive as their reward, realizing it meant a small fortune to them, and tried to infer that we should not be welcomed on Pulo Taratau. At last, after hours of wrangling, they agreed to take us to Langkawi for the sum of $60, and we heaved an audible sigh of relief. It was all fixed, so we should be back amongst our own folk and, even more important, be able to announce our survival to our grief stricken families at home.

We were given another meal of rice and dried fish, washed down with the delicious coconut milk and, at midday, we were escorted down the beach to the sea-going sampan, a 35 foot open boat already manned by her crew of five. We said goodbye to our benefactors, now openly friendly, and waved to the villagers gathered on the beach to see us off. The large single bamboo-laced sail was hauled up the mast and, with a following breeze, we turned our backs on Pulo Nipis and sailed eastwards towards civilization.

As the sun sank in the west, the outline of our island appeared on the dark horizon and we sailed on into the night. The breeze freshened and the sampan buried her bows into the swell and rolled alarmingly, throwing up a beautiful iridescence in her wake. The deck boards were painful to our protruding bones but the joy in our hearts transcended any physical discomfort that we suffered. One of the fishermen boiled rice over a small brazier on the deck and this, with more dried fish helped down by weak tea, provided our evening meal.

Our difficult conversation lagged and we tried to settle down to sleep, but we were frozen stiff in the chilly night air. The first glimmer of dawn silhouetted the island before us. A certain amount of anxiety had remained within us as we could not be quite certain that our rescuers would adhere to their bargain, but the outline of the island brought relief from our fears as we recognized the wooded hills of Langkawi.

Day Seven – Thursday 11 April

On this day a personal notice appeared in the *Birmingham Post* announcing the death of Flying Officer Charles Harley Boxall. The family must have been thrown into emotional turmoil when, during the evening, a telegram arrived from the Air Ministry saying that Harley was alive and well.

> IMMEDIATE FROM AIR MINISTRY VERY PLEASED TO TELL YOU THAT INFORMATION RECEIVED FROM FAR EAST STATES YOUR SON WAS PICKED UP NOT INJURED AND WELL STOP. NOW AT ALOR STAR.

We anchored off the island-studded narrows until the sun had risen and then, hoisting the sail, we moved up between the islands on the last ten-mile stretch to the village of Kuah which was the main settlement. With the tying up of the boat against the wooden jetty, we knew that our tribulations were over. I clambered up on to the landing stage and tottered ashore. I saw the Union Jack flying on a tall flagstaff outside the Government buildings and went in and asked for the district officer. A startled Malay clerk led me into the presence of this official. I briefly told him our story and asked him to send off signals over his radio transmitter to RAF Singapore, Tengah and Alor Star.

He was most kind and placed a pad and pencil on the desk before me. I wrote out my message, stating that we had been picked up uninjured and well. This culminating action snapped the last thread of my self-control. My heart burst within me, and I wept. I was glad Rodger and Martin were not in the room, to witness this moment of weakness.

The district officer was kindness itself. He got my signals off without delay, paid the $60 to the men who had restored us to civilization and arranged for the medical officer to dress Martin's leg, fortunately kept healthy by the frequent immersion in salt water. A large meal was prepared for us, but somehow we did not feel very hungry. He provided soap and razors but, before removing the growth of beard, he asked that he be allowed to take our photographs, promising to send on copies to us, to which we readily assented.

It was a Thursday, the 11 April, and it transpired that we had arrived on a fortuitous day as the weekly steamer was leaving Langkawi for Alor Star that morning. The district officer had a huge hamper prepared for our remaining 8-hour sea trip and this is what we discovered later on board that he had put in for our sustenance:

1lb loaves of bread
1 tin of butter
2 tins of bully beef
1 tin of fruit salad
1 packet of cheese
50 cigarettes
6 boxes of matches
6 bottles of beer
6 bottles of orangeade

All this for three people for an 8-hour journey – we were obviously not meant to starve. After much hand shaking, heartfelt thanks from us and good wishes from the district officer and his colleagues, we boarded the coastal steamer at 1030 on the last leg of our journey home. The day passed peacefully enough, steaming across the shining waters, but we could not make much impression on our food hamper.

With the glorious setting of the sun, we entered Kuala Kedah, the fishing village near Alor Star, and tied up at the jetty. Our friends were waiting for us. It seemed that the whole village and the whole population of Alor Star had turned out to greet us; but we did not notice this very much, our hearts being too full with the miracle of restoration to life. We returned to the guesthouse at Kapala Batas. After a glorious hot bath and a meal, I turned in early and sank into the luxury of a bed. The following afternoon, Rodger, Martin and I were put on the train and, after an overnight journey, arrived at Singapore the next evening. My squadron commander met us at the railway station and we returned to Tengah. Rodger and Martin got out of the car at the Sergeants' Mess; we clasped hands in silent recognition of the bond which had been forged between us.

My CO and I went on to the Mess where there was quite a reception awaiting me. My friends were all for making a party of it, but the Doc intervened and led me off to my room where he gave me a cursory examination and told me to take things easy. I soon drifted into a peaceful sleep, silently agreeing with the remarks of one of my friends who said: 'You have had all the fun since we have been out here – Khota Bahru, Alor Star, wrecked on a desert island…' I certainly had had all the fun, but also the anxiety which this last episode had caused to my family, the shock, the suspense and grief especially to my father who was already a partial invalid with heart trouble.

The following day the Doc gave me a through medical examination. He could not find anything organically wrong except a general weakness as the result of privations, but he put me off flying for the time being and I filled in the time with my Mess secretarial duties.

Despite Harley being safe and well on 12 April he was listed in the RAF's 25th Casualty Report and was still reported as missing. The names of his two crew, Rodger 58025 Sergeant and Martin 563352 LAC, were given in the same list.

Saturday 13 April

On what would have been day nine of Harley's ordeal if he and his crew had not been rescued, a report appeared in the *Birmingham Post* with the headlines, 'Good News For Handsworth Family – Flying Officer Not Dead As Reported'.

The story read:

> One of the happiest homes in Birmingham yesterday was that of Mr and Mrs J.E. Boxall, 9 Ivy Road, Handsworth, Birmingham, where it became possible to abandon mourning.
>
> On Friday of last week Mr and Mrs Boxall were informed by the Air Ministry that their son, Flying Officer Charles Harley Boxall, on service with the RAF in the East, was missing, but that a search for him was in progress. On Tuesday they learned that the search had been abandoned and Thursday's issue of the *Birmingham Post* contained an advertisement of his death. In an official casualty list published on Thursday night Flying Officer Boxall was posted as missing.
>
> But yesterday Mr Boxall received a telegram informing him that his son had been picked up hundreds of miles from his base, safe and well.

Subsequent Events

By the 16 April Harley was back at RAF Tengah and he wrote to his family to explain what had happened.

My Dear Dad, Mater and Duncan,

Yesterday I received your cable and one from Geoff. So now you now that everything is O.K. I returned to Tengah on Sunday (14th). It is a little difficult to know how to write a letter having faced death twice within one week, firstly by drowning and secondly by starvation!

But I know that you must all be waiting with interest the details of our (me, my air observer and my wireless operator) experience so I will set to straight away and record the bare facts in chronological order.

What followed was a detailed account of events leading up to the forced landing and Harley's time on the island, much of which has already been described. Although Harley's brother Duncan is mentioned in the letter he was already serving in the army and was stationed in the Orkneys. The final paragraph read:

I am now feeling quite well although still a little weak and I am having a thorough medical examination before recommencing work. Had to tell the whole story to the Air Vice Marshal, AOC Far East Command yesterday and spent the whole day on Court of Inquiry. Many thanks for your No. 32 Dad and your holiday snap of Duncan. Will reply fully in next letter. Hope you three are all keeping fit – sorry to have given you so much anxiety. Love and best wishes to all three and Gwen. Your affectionate Harley.

Harley might have appeared before the AOC on 15 April but that was only for a preliminary interview for his actions to be considered prior to any disciplinary charges being made. The main hearing was at a Court of Inquiry but that was not held until July.

CHAPTER 8

The Aftermath

Early in May, whilst still on sick leave, I had a most enjoyable ten days in Penang, My friend, Eric, and I boarded a coastal steamer of 1,400 tons in Singapore harbour and sailed up the west coast to the Malay Peninsula. We were the only passengers on board although there were forty-eight 1st class berths. On the way we called in at Port Swettenham and Telok Anson, thirty miles up the estuary, to discharge and take on cargo and, after three days, arrived at the island of Penang.

By cable car we climbed Government Hill for an overall look at this 'Pearl of the Orient'. In all directions verdant hills rolled to the sea. Junks, freighters, and green islets, half obscured by mist, flecked the opalescent waters. The pink roofs of Georgetown, the island's metropolis, covered a finger like a peninsula pointing at the mainland.

In a small English car we drove the scenic road which girdles the island. Penang, we discovered, is Malaya in miniature. Coconut groves, paddy fields and vegetable gardens cover small lowland areas; rubber trees and jungle clothe steep hillsides. Busy Chinese hamlets straddle the road and Malay villages of carved wooden bungalows stand on stilts, before graceful palms. Georgetown, with its modern hotels, stores, banks suburbs and crowded harbour seems like a smaller Singapore.

The tourist guide books are not far wrong when they call it The Brightest Gem In The Orient – marvellous sandy beaches with coconut palms down to the water's edge, the contours of the island rising in hills and valleys to a height of 2,700 feet, profuse with lush jungle vegetation. We booked in at the P & O Hotel in Georgetown, the capital, and it was there that we learned that a P & O liner carrying the wives of our squadron officers had just docked on its way to Singapore. We went along and met them.

They were amazed when they saw me as the last they had heard, from their husbands, was that I had been reported missing; in fact, one poor girl nearly fainted but we took her along to the hotel and revived her with several gin-slings. They left that afternoon on the last leg of their journey for a happy reunion with their respective husbands after eight months' separation.

Eric and I hired a car at $3. 30 (7/9) per day for the duration of our stay, which enabled us to explore the whole island and, incidentally, saved a lot of money in taxi fares. We visited the Buddhist temple and monastery at Aya Itam (Holy Water) and spent two hours with our priestly guide, round the gardens where the holy turtles are kept, into the temple where we witnessed a service in progress and up 257 steps to the minaret. We took tea with the monks and were informed that for the sum of $500 one's photograph could be hung in the temple.

We motored on to the foot of the hills and took a mountain train to the summit, mostly at a gradient of 1 in 2. It was wonderfully cool and refreshing up there, giving a marvellous view of the island and the Malay peninsula fifteen miles to the east. We had a drink at the hotel – an ideal place for a honeymoon – and as the lights of Georgetown twinkled below made our descent in the darkness.

The few days past quickly. Most mornings we would go along to the swimming club, who graciously made us honorary members for our stay and, in the afternoons, explored more of the island in our little Morris. In the evenings, we would go along to one of the cabarets , buy a string of tickets and while away the hours with the pretty little Malay, Chinese and Eurasian taxi-dancers to the haunting tunes of 'easternized' jazz. Being in mufti and incognito we could indulge in these pleasures; not so in Singapore where such diversions were out-of-bounds to commissioned ranks. We boarded the steamer in Penang harbour and after a pleasant three-day trip returned to Singapore.

At the end of May, I had another medical board and was pronounced fit, but the doctors insisted on another twenty-one days' sick leave before returning to flying duties. My wireless operator also passed his medical examination, but Rodger was boarded for return to the United Kingdom.

Harley had the first of two medical boards on 24 May in Singapore and it was found that he was still suffering from shock and exposure. His medical category was downgraded and he was referred to another board on 16 June. He was then found to be fit enough to return to 62 Squadron for flying duties and his previous medical status was restored.

As for the other two members of Harley's crew they fared very differently. LAC Martin remained with 62 Squadron on flying duties and was later promoted to sergeant. Sergeant Rodger was badly affected by the incident and he returned to the home establishment. He was later hospitalized after he was found to be suffering from severe stress and mental health problems.

Having been found guilty by the Court of Inquiry for the loss of an aeroplane, Harley was summarily tried on 1 July, by the AOC Far East, Air Vice-Marshal John Tremayne Babbington.

The AOC, who was 49 years old, had joined the Royal Navy in 1908 as a midshipman and, after being commissioned in 1911, had risen rapidly through the ranks. In 1919 he was listed as a major but was removed from the Navy List after being awarded a permanent commission in the RAF. He had taken over as AOC Far East in 1938 and his appointments prior to that had mainly involved training and diplomacy. He came from a privileged background and represented the old school of tradition and naval discipline. Those who came before him could not expect to get off lightly.

I have moved forward the text concerning Harley's comments on the Court of Inquiry, so that they are in a more appropriate place in his story.

The usual Court of Inquiry was convened at which evidence was taken to ascertain the cause of the accident. The cause was obvious, I think, that an aircraft will not stay in the air when the engines have ceased to function. But I was very surprised when, a week later, I was summoned before my station commander who informed me that air headquarters had presented charges against me for the loss of one of His Majesty's aircraft and that I was to appear before the AOC the following day.

He handed me a typewritten sheet enumerating the three charges: As captain of the aircraft (1) failing to ensure the proper navigation of the aircraft, (2) failing to ensure that the proper navigational equipment was carried in the aircraft, (3) failing to ensure that the water can was filled before flight. There is no doubt that I was technically guilty of all charges and, as captain of the aircraft, was responsible for these omissions; but I could not help feeling that the ultimate result, the aircraft crashing due to engine failure, was not attributable to any of these technical offences.

In fact as far as the faulty navigation equipment was concerned, I felt that we had been extremely fortunate in being off our course which had brought us near an island when the second engine failed, otherwise we would have ditched in the sea, 100 miles from land, with the problematical chance of survival. I could hardly believe that such charges could be made against me after all we had been through, the attempt to accomplish the mission on one engine and the difficulties with which we had had to contend. My station commander was most sympathetic and he told me that he had done everything in his power to have the charges quashed, but without success.

In company with my squadron commander, I presented myself before the AOC, RAF Far East, the following morning. The charges were read out to me and the AOC asked me if I had anything to say, as he had decided to deal with the matter summarily, in other words, I was not to have the option of trial by court martial.

I said:

Sir, I plead guilty to the charges against me but before making your judgement I would ask you to take into consideration my past record. Since I joined the service it has been my ambition to obtain a permanent commission and I feel that any black mark on my service record will seriously prejudice my chances.

The AOC delivered his judgement: 'Severe reprimand'. I saluted and marched out of his office. I have always been one for discipline and I have never questioned orders from my superior officers but, I am sorry to say that I have never become reconciled to this punishment.

There may have been a number of facts that influenced the AOC's decision to award Harley a severe reprimand, one of them being that he had previously been involved with the loss of another Blenheim in November 1938. Although Harley had been found not to blame on that occasion, the slightest suspicion of negligence on his part, whether recent or in the past, might have contributed to the AOC not giving him the benefit of the doubt.

However it may have been that one particular incident influenced the AOC in his judgement and on 8 April, just four days after Harley's aircraft had gone missing, another 62 Squadron Blenheim was lost. Sergeant Syd Stafford and his crew of Sergeants Bury and Warwick survived when their aircraft force landed in the jungle near Sabang in Siam. It is not clear what caused the crash but it is understood that the engines seized up in a similar manner to those on Harley's Blenheim. The loss of two aircraft in a matter of four days would have caused concern amongst the air staff, especially as the Air Ministry in London had recently been refused an increase in air strength.

Sergeant Stafford and his crew were subsequently interned by the controlling Dutch authorities but were released a few weeks later when Holland entered the war. We do not know what punishment Sergeant Stafford suffered as a result of losing an aircraft, or if he was disciplined at all, but it is possible that Harley's severe reprimand was awarded to set an example.

At this time the Nazis invaded Holland and Belgium, with two minor repercussions in our part of the world: one of the German merchantmen which we had bottled up in

Sabang harbour scuttled herself and one of our squadron crews, a sergeant pilot with his navigator and wireless operator, who had force landed in Sumatra on a similar photographic reconnaissance a few days after our own effort, were restored to us after what appeared to have been, from the stories they told, a most enjoyable holiday.

These events were quickly followed by the entry of Italy into the war, and the stunning news of the collapse of France. Air raids over East Anglia intensified and the political situation in the Far East deteriorated.

After ten weeks on the ground, I was pronounced fit for full flying duties and returned to my flight as second in command, assuming full command as my flight commander was off sick. It was good to be in the air again and, if anything, the experience of my forced landing had given me increased confidence; I felt that, having got away with the island episode, I could face up to any perils the future might have in store for me.

Hitler's peace offensive in July was followed by the heaviest air raids by the Luftwaffe, culminating in the glorious Battle of Britain. We, in the Far East, could only count the score and pursue the casualty list, in almost every one recognizing the names of our friends. The mounting sense of frustration on our part was tempered only by the time spent in continuous stand-by duty and the fact that we were in the air many hours of daylight and darkness, taking part in exercises to test the AA defences of Singapore.

In early September, at the time of the entry of the Japanese into Indo-China, I flew up to Alor Star to assume command of a detachment in occupation of the airfield. This was my first independent command and I felt very bucked, especially as I was taking over from a squadron leader. The detachment consisted of a score of airmen and my main duty was to prepare the station for occupation by a squadron and to assist the Army to perfect the defences against ground forces.

The place had changed considerably since my last visit five months before. Barrack blocks and messes had been built, another hangar erected and earthworks thrown up, three sided 'pens' for the protection of aircraft against bomb blast. There was still a considerable amount of work to be done but I was fortunate in having a very conscientious and cheerful clerk of works from the Air Ministry Works Directorate and the help and understanding of the Malayan civil service officials with whom, I gathered, I had acquired a certain amount of notoriety as a result of my island adventure.

In addition to RAF personnel, I also had under my command a detachment from the Keddah Police, a dozen swarthy Indian Sikhs, who provided the airfield guard. Later when the Indian Army took up quarters in the vicinity, a company of the Bhahalpur Rifles augmented the garrison. I was the only RAF officer on the station and fulfilled all duties from being station commander downwards. Cipher messages coming in at all hours of the day and night kept me very busy.

The detachment mentioned below was of Lockheed Hudson aircraft of 21 Squadron Royal Australian Air Force. They were regular visitors to Alor Star as were aircraft from a number of other RAF units.

For the next few months, detachments of three aircraft from the RAAF squadron in Singapore spent a week at a time at Alor Star and, although they provided more work for me, particularly in the messing arrangements, they provided good company. But life was not all work. We used to play a fair amount of tennis at the Keddah Club in the short evenings. We were honorary members of the club which provided a golf course, tennis courts and a billiard room and the monthly dance was well patronized.

PART TWO

CHAPTER 1

Alor Star

Because of ill health Harley was unable to continue writing his memoirs and it is at this point that his own personal story ends and my account (Joe Bamford), of his life begins.

After he had been disciplined by the AOC over the desert island incident, Harley was quite concerned about his future in the RAF but it turned out that his anxiety was not justified. In September 1940 he was promoted to flight lieutenant and given command of the RAF Station at Alor Star in Malaya.

Alor Star is a seaport situated on the River Keddah and during the 1930s the town had a population of 11,600. The airfield had a tarmac runway that was 3,000 feet long that ran from north-east to south-west and two shorter grass strips on an area 2,700 feet by 3,000 feet. Over the years it had played host to a number of famous aviators, including Jean Batten who landed there on 20 May 1934, on what turned out to be a record breaking flight from Britain to Australia.

Harley arrived at Alor Star on 28 September and took over command from Squadron Leader John Duncan, who was soon to become the CO of 62 Squadron. It was an important station that was connected with other RAF airfields such as those at Kuanton and Kota Bharu via the inter command W/T station, and the communications chain was a vital link for the defence of the region.

One of the first things that Harley had to do after his arrival was to write a report, in response to a request from Far East Air Force HQ, about the dispersal and concealment of aircraft on the airfield. By 3 October he had produced a detailed report that pointed out where improvements were needed, but he made it abundantly clear how bad the situation was. Only if sufficient warning of an air attack was made, was there any hope of protecting the aircraft, by getting them airborne as soon as possible. By the beginning of December the first hangar had been built at Alor Star with the use of 35,000 sandbags but the location of a Bellman hangar and most of the aircraft pens was still under consideration.

Back at Tengah meanwhile, 62 Squadron was involved in a number of bombing, photographic and formation exercises but there was no flying at all between 10 – 13 December because the aerodrome was unserviceable after very heavy rain had fallen. On the 23rd Squadron Leader Lawrence Victor Spencer (later Wing Commander, OBE) who, at some point in 1940, had taken over command of 62 Squadron from Wing Commander Farnhill, was posted to Seletar to take up a role involving training. When Squadron Leader John Duncan became the new CO he was posted in from headquarters at Tengah.

During the New Year of 1941 correspondence about defence measures continued to arrive from AHQ and it was decided that a total of thirty-two aircraft pens were required at Alor Star. It was suggested that they be built on the north side of the airfield away from the technical and domestic areas but Harley had other ideas. He thought that they should be built on what was considered to be bad ground in the middle of the three grass runways. AHQ agreed with him but Harley had many other decisions to make concerning the positioning of air raid shelters and protection for ground crews.

On 2 February he held a meeting with Dr R.A. Beattie, the medical officer for north Keddah, to discuss the hospitalization and clearing of war casualties, should that situation ever arise. These preparations and meetings contradict the claims of a number of authors who have said that the Far East Air Force was totally unprepared for war with Japan.

On the same day that Harley met Dr Beattie, he handed over command of Alor Star to Wing Commander R.G. Forbes, although he remained on the station but assumed his old duties as the adjutant. The changes were made in advance of 62 Squadron's move from Tengah to Alor Star, under its new CO. The main reason for 62 Squadron pulling out of Tengah was that the airfield was regularly unserviceable and through much of January 1941 it had been flooded by heavy rain. A new 2,500 feet metalled runway was to be laid down and the building work would cause a lot of disruption to RAF operations.

Station headquarters at RAF Alor Star officially opened on 1 February and the movement order No. 3, dated 3 February 1941, noted that the advance party consisted of two junior officers and two senior NCOs. They were posted to Alor Star on 5 February but the main party of ground personnel and the air party did not arrive for another month.

Not all survived long enough to make the move to Alor Star and on 24 February Flight Lieutenant Halliwell and two of his crew were killed when Blenheim L1104, crashed at Sungei Patani. The accident happened after an engine had suddenly cut out and rather remarkably Sergeant Hayes, who was in the bomb well, somehow survived. Although Flight Lieutenant Halliwell also survived the initial impact, he died soon afterwards of his injuries. The other two members of his crew were Sergeants Walker and Couzens who were both married. All three airmen were buried in Taiping War Cemetery in Malaya.

The aircraft of 62 Squadron moved from Tengah to Alor Star on 10 March but, as he was still carrying out the duties of the adjutant, Harley was not one of the pilots named in the air party. The names of those who were on the original nominal roll, dated 21 January 1941, are mentioned below and are an accurate record of those who served on 62 Squadron at this time. In just a few short months many of them would be dead and the list was compiled before the accident which killed Flight Lieutenant Halliwell and his crew.

Nominal Roll Of Air Party For Move To Alor Star

1. L1432 S/L. Duncan, Sgt. Wooley, Sgt. Langham, Cpl. Brighton

2. L1134 F/Lt. Keegan, Sgt. Bere,* Sgt. Ball, Cpl. O'Neill

3. L1243 Sgt. Dawson,* Sgt. Brown, Sgt. Clifton, Cpl. Smith

4. L1103 F/O. Henderson, Sgt. Reynolds, Sgt. Dutton, Cpl. Blewitt

5. L1104 F/O. Halliwell,* Sgt. Walker,* Sgt. Couzens,* Cpl.

Freeman

6. L1346 F/Lt. Scarf,* Sgt. Calder, Sgt. Rich, Cpl. Thomas

7. L1253 Fl/Lt. Irving, Sgt. Brinndler, Sgt. Wilcox, Sgt. Barton

8. L1259 F/Lt. Lancaster,* Sgt. Metcalfe, Sgt. Oliver,* Cpl Miller

9. L1256 F/Lt. Hutchins, Sgt. Still, Sgt. Quinn, F/Sgt. Seaband

10. L7173 F/O. Fish, Sgt. Powell,* Sgt. Templteton,* Cpl. Leather

11. L1349 F/O. Frostick, Sgt. Brown, Sgt. Cameron, Sgt. Grice

12. L1107 F/Lt. Pattison, Sgt. Bowie,* Sgt Martin,* Cpl. Lane-Ryan

13. L1132 P/O. Haigh,* Sgt. Warwick, Sgt. Wills, Cpl. Wilkinson

14. L3442 Sgt. Stafford,* Sgt. Willmott, Sgt. Hicks, Sgt. Spooner

* Indicates those that died either on air operations 1941/44 or in other circumstances.

On the day of the move from Tengah, the aircraft took-off at 0800 under the leadership of Squadron Leader Duncan. They flew out over Malaya via Port Swettenham and landed at Alor Star at 1030 to begin a new chapter in the squadron's history.

In March Harley was appointed as 'B' flight commander which presumably meant that he was able to give up the position of adjutant which he had filled, on and off, for over three years. Despite that he was not one of the pilots that were sent on a detachment to Mergui in Siam, which involved a total of twelve aircraft and forty-nine personnel. His absence from the records at this time suggest that he may have been on leave or on detachment to AHQ at Tengah, the dates of which are not known.

On 5 April, Wing Commander Geoff Farnhill, the former CO of 62 Squadron, who had written to Harley's father when he was presumed lost, was killed in what can only be described as a bizarre accident. The day before three Blenheims of 27 Squadron had collided while performing aerobatics and two ended up crashing into the sea. Wing Commander Farnhill was the commander of a launch called the *Buffalo* and the following morning, when it went out to search for survivors, the boat ran into a minefield and exploded. There were approximately twenty airmen from 151 Maintenance Unit on board the boat but there were no survivors.

It seems that some time after arriving in the Far East Harley had overcome the grief of being separated from his beloved Maureen, whom he had left behind in England. In early 1941 he met his future wife, an Australian nurse who was working in The Queen Alexandra's Imperial Nursing Service that had been formed as early as 1854. Patricia Davies, who came from Perth in Western Australia, was the daughter of Chief Justice Thomas Davies, who was a High Court Judge. He wanted Pat to study law and become a lawyer but much to his disappointment she trained as a nurse instead and studied general nursing practice and midwifery at Perth Hospital.

Pat remained in Perth until 1938 when she decide to travel overseas and went to work at the Alexandria Hospital in Singapore, before moving on to hospitals in Kuala Lumpur, Seramban and Alor Star, where she met Harley. We do not know the date or circumstances of her first meeting with Harley but it was probably just after he arrived in the town in September. Pat Davies was five years older than 28 year old Harley but he was much more mature than his age suggests. They were married on 19 May 1941 at Keddah Registry Office and one of Pat's bridesmaids was Sister Alethea Gentles, while the best man was Flight Lieutenant Norman Irving.

Flight Lieutenant Irving had married the year before and he may have set a precedence, because not only did Harley marry Pat Davies, but soon afterwards Pongo Scarf was married to Elizabeth Norah Mary Lunn, another nurse who was working in the Queen Alexandra Nursing Service. The common bond between them was that they both came from Wimbledon and when Elizabeth first met Pongo she discovered that back in England she had walked past his home every day on her way to work. Elizabeth was actually known as Sallie, but the reason for the change of name is not known and the source of some speculation. Sallie Hammond, Sallie Scarf's goddaughter, has suggested that she was given the name when she was going through nursing training, maybe because there was already another Elizabeth working in the same place. That, however, has not been confirmed.

Both Harley and Pongo were among the most popular officers on the squadron and it has been claimed that some of the officers were most unpopular. A number of former ground crew claim that there was a lot of snobbery between aircrew, and particularly some officers and those airmen who served in the ranks. Stan Fielding, who was an aircraft fitter, claimed that in the three years he served on 62 Squadron the pilot of the aircraft that he serviced never spoke directly to him. Orders were passed down the line from pilot to the sergeant in charge of the ground crew, to corporal and then to an airman.

In June 1941, 62 Squadron took part in a number of tactical exercises and by this time Harley was flying more regularly because he handed over the role of adjutant to another officer. His regular Blenheim L1260, carried the code letter 'O' and his crew consisted of Sergeants Martin and Steel. Martin was a long serving member of Harley's crew who had shared the experience of the desert island with him, while Steel was a newcomer. Most of the exercises involved practice squadron formation take-offs, mock bombing attacks on Singapore and joint operations with the Royal Navy searching for German shipping.

In July Harley took part in a number of cross-country and night-flying exercises and on the 16th he flew as number four on a round robin exercise, of a 'six ship' lead by Pongo Scarf that was routed via Ipoh, Butterworth and Penang. On the 31st he took part in an early morning night-flying exercise and flew as number three in a formation lead by Flight Lieutenant Keegan. On both these occasions he flew with his regular crew, whose wireless operator varied between Sergeant Quinn and Sergeant Martin.

There were continuous exercises in the months leading up to the Japanese invasion of Malaya, including mock bombing attacks on Alor Star and night-flying training at Sungei Patani. There was a practice armament camp at Kunaton in the middle of October but

Harley did not take part in any of the sorties. In the same month he was promoted to the acting rank of squadron leader and he was by then one of the most experienced officers on the squadron.

At the beginning of December there were a number of changes to the command structure and the CO of 62 Squadron, Wing Commander Duncan, also took command of the station at Alor Star. Harley's rank was again changed to temporary squadron leader. Pongo Scarf and Flight Lieutenant Keegan were also made up to squadron leader.

One the eve of the Japanese invasion, the strength of the establishment of 62 Squadron was twelve pilots, including Harley, who was still a flight commander when he was appointed as acting squadron commander. Most of the senior NCO pilots and aircrew were promoted to flight sergeant and by the end of the campaign many of them has risen to the rank of warrant officer.

Officer Commanding: Wing Commander John Duncan (34151)

Flight Commander & Acting Squadron Commander: Squadron Leader C.H. Boxall.

Flight Commander: Squadron Leader E.A. Keegan (37679)

Pilots: Squadron Leader A.S.K. Scarf; Flight Lieutenant N.R. Irving; Flight Lieutenant N.D. Lancaster; Flight Lieutenant H.J. Fish; Flight Lieutenant W.A. Pattison; Flight Lieutenant D.M. Frostick; Flying Officer Haigh; Sergeant S Stafford; Sergeant Dawson

On 1 December 1941 Far East Command declared No. 2 state of readiness and five days later, when the Japanese fleet was sighted off the coast of Siam, No. 1 state of readiness. The strength of 62 Squadron was eleven Blenheims.

Pongo Scarf is not listed as having any specific responsibilities but regardless of that it was he who accompanied Harley on 7 December in an attempt to intercept a Japanese reconnaissance aircraft that had flown over Alor Star on several occasions. The Japanese aircraft was flying far too high for two old Blenheims to catch and so Harley and Pongo returned to base feeling rather frustrated.

The following day however, 62 Squadron flew on what Harley later described as the first and only operation that it carried out as a unit, when he led eleven Blenheims to bomb the Japanese invasion fleet. They took off at 0900 and after flying over Kota Bharu and failing to see any Japanese aircraft on the ground, they continued on to the coast of Siam. Near Patani Harley observed a number of Japanese ships and landing craft, and each Blenheim dropped two 500 lb bombs from 8,000 feet, encountering only moderate anti-aircraft fire.

It is possible that by bombing the Japanese fleet off the coast of Siam, Harley and his fellow officers may have contravened orders given by the British Minister in Siam, Sir Josiah Crosby. He had ruled that British forces were not to attack or occupy any part of Siam until Japan had struck the first blow and despite the fact that that had already happened, it is doubtful if his order had been rescinded. At the time Air Force HQ was almost certainly unaware of the secret pact in which Siam had agreed it would provide Japan with landing beaches and support, for the price of its own neutrality.

Against the odds all of 62 Squadron's aircraft and crews returned to Alor Star safely but approximately thirty minutes after they had landed, and while the Blenheims were still being rearmed and refuelled, the Japanese attacked the airfield. A force of about twenty-seven enemy aircraft bombed Alor Star, completely destroying at least three Blenheims and rendering another three damaged and unserviceable. Three airman were killed on the ground, the most senior of them being the adjutant, Flying Officer Crossley Cooke, who came from Cobham and who had only recently married. Just minutes before the raid it is claimed that Cooke had spoken to Captain Patrick Stanley Heenan, an English officer who came from Cheam in Surrey, but was of Irish descent, and who had sympathies with the Republican movement. Heenan had only recently arrived in the Far East and he had been seconded to the 16th Punjab Regiment.

On the fateful day, Cooke is claimed to have commented: 'I cannot understand why the Japanese have bombed everywhere else and left Alor Star alone.'

Heenan is said to have replied confidently: 'Oh they will come,' and of that he was certain because he had just informed the Japanese by a secret radio that 62 Squadron was on the ground. He had given the enemy the codes of the day and all the information about aircraft types, numbers available and anything else they needed to be able to attack Alor Star and other RAF bases.

On 9 December there was a certain amount of sabotage caused by locals, who were probably members of Heenan's organization and the airfield at Alor Star was abandoned. It had also been badly damaged by the bombing and the petrol dump destroyed and so 62 Squadron was ordered to move south to Butterworth. Out of the original eleven Blenheims that had flown the day before, only six of 62 Squadron's aircraft were serviceable enough to be flown out. The airfield at Butterworth is situated on the mainland opposite the island of Penang and there it was joined by the remnants of 27, 34 and 60 Squadrons.

Almost as soon as they arrived at Butterworth orders were received that all available aircraft were to carry out an attack on the Japanese occupied airfield of Singora in Siam. The story of what happened this day, and particularly the actions of Squadron Leader Arthur 'Pongo' Scarf, has been told many times in different books and publications. He took off in his Blenheim, L1134, with his navigator, Flight Sergeant Paddy Calder and wireless operator, Flight Sergeant Cyril Rich. They were the only crew able to do so because just as they took-off the Japanese bombed Butterworth and caused a lot of damage, preventing other aircraft from becoming airborne.

A number of those pilots and aircrew who were getting ready to take-off were killed or seriously wounded and amongst the dead was Flight Sergeant Willis who was in the crew of Flying Officer Frostick. Frostick was wounded in his arm and shoulder but he was saved from more serious injury by the parachute pack of his observer. Flight Sergeant John Lewis Francis Willis from Northern Ireland was not so fortunate and he was killed

Despite the fact that his was the only aircraft left in the air, Pongo decided to continue with his mission, ignoring the fact that it had been planned as a squadron attack. Rather remarkably Pongo reached

Singora and dropped his bombs but soon afterwards his aircraft came under repeated attack by Japanese fighters and he was badly wounded in the arm and back. With the help of the other two members of his crew Pongo managed to maintain control but he knew that he would not be able to get back to Butterworth and he would have to make a forced landing. When he observed that they were passing directly over Alor Star, Pongo he made a decision to try and put down there. Whether it was because he was too badly wounded to carry on or because by some subconscious instinct he knew that his wife Sallie was there, and he would see her at the end, we shall never know!

The Blenheim made a forced landing in a paddy field just a short distance from the hospital and with the help of his crew he was lifted out of the wreck of the aircraft. A number of people from the hospital ran to the scene and Pongo was soon in the hospital undergoing treatment and fighting for his life.

Despite what has been said and written about how Pongo died, one thing is certain; his wife Sallie was present when he arrived at the hospital and along with Squadron Leader Boxall's wife Pat, she was amongst the staff that treated him. Pat set up an intravenous drip and Sallie gave her husband a blood transfusion, while they waited for him to be taken into theatre.

Sallie later recalled the events of what happened in some detail:

On 9 December 1941 I was off duty when Pat, another nursing sister at Alor Star Hospital, said an English patient was being brought in.

I was very shocked when I discovered that the patient was my husband Pongo, who by some miracle had managed to land his plane in a paddy field nearby to the aerodrome and hospital, his two sergeants being Rich and Calder. Dr Peach, who had brought him in had administered some medication and Pongo was saying cheerfully, 'Don't worry', but he was severely wounded in his left arm and back. He was quietly settled in a twin bedded ward and a saline drip was put up by his bed. As soon as the Asian doctor saw him he ordered at least two pints of blood. As I was compatible two pints were taken.

When I came over Dr Peach was there with Rich and Calder. He told me about Pongo's arm and I felt very depressed when I heard it was his left one, as he was left handed and he had once said to me that flying was his whole life and I thought how is he going to manage if he can't fly? Then when he was moved from the stretcher the severe wound in his back bled profusely and we gave him two pints of blood. What cheered me up was when I heard him saying, 'Now Pat, don't get fresh with my mammary glands'.

Pat Boxall went with him to theatre. Pongo was still conscious and said, 'Don't worry, keep smiling. Chin up!' Pat returned soon afterwards and told me that he had slipped away under anaesthesia. I couldn't believe it and went to theatre to verify the tragic news. The next day Pat's husband, Squadron Leader Harley Boxall and Norman Irving arrived and took us to join the other European wives and children for evacuation.

But I returned to Alor Star by cadging a lift in a lorry and picked up my uniform and a few personal items. The whole place looked quite desolate and I must thank Phyllis Briggs (she remained behind) for burying my late husband. I was indeed very lucky to finally leave Alor Star.

The evacuation of 62 Squadron's personnel from Alor Star began on 10 December and the airfield was finally abandoned on the 14th. Most airmen and officers, including Harley, travelled by road to Taiping, where 62 Squadron was reforming. Some later completed the journey to Ipoh in lorries, while others continued to Singapore by rail. The ensuing days brought only chaos and panic during a hurried retreat.

On the night of 13 December, Group Captain R.G. Forbes, who had previously commanded Alor Star and more recently RAF Butterworth, called for volunteers. He urgently wanted three pilots to fly some American built Brewster Buffalo fighters out of Butterworth to Ipoh and Harley, Flight Lieutenant Lancaster and Sergeant Sid Stafford volunteered for the job.

The three airmen had only recently arrived at Taiping and they had to drive right through the night to get to Butterworth, where they then had to familiarize themselves with the cockpit layout and pilot's notes. Despite the fact that none of them had previously flown the Buffalo and they had no recent experience of modern single-engined fighters, they managed to deliver all three safely during the morning of the 14th where they joined others from 453 and 21 RAAF Squadrons.

After reporting to headquarters at Ipoh, Harley and a number of other officers were ordered to carry out a rather unusual task for experienced aircrew. Because they were technically redundant and had no aircraft to fly they were given three armoured cars, known as AFVs and ordered to participate in a vital rearguard action. Between 15-17 December Harley's armoured vehicle patrolled a sixty-mile section of the Grik Road that ran from Kuala Kangsar. There was great concern that the Japanese would overrun the airfield at Taiping in a pincer movement and the role of the AFV crews was to slow them down and support the British forces that were trying to retreat down the road to Singapore.

Harley was put in charge of the operation and his patrols did not pass without incident because forty-five miles up the Grik Road his AFV came across a section of the Argyle and Sutherland Highlanders, who were fighting a rearguard action and were being closely pursued by Japanese troops. When Harley asked the sergeant major how long he should stay on the road to support them, he shouted out: 'Until the ******* Japanese arrive!'

It may have been that Harley was quite stunned by his sudden change in fortune and, as he stood in the gun turret, he pondered on how he had effectively become part of the army. He was the vehicle commander and the gunner, while the air gunner fed the guns and the bomb aimer was the driver. So as to make a hasty retreat if it was required, Harley ordered the AFV to be turned around, so that the rear of the vehicle faced down the road. That also gave Harley a clearer field of fire of between 150 and 200 yards towards the direction from which the enemy were expected.

While they waited for the Japanese to show up, the metal hull of the vehicle absorbed the sweltering heat and after a while Harley and his crew began to feel very hot and tircd. Then all of a sudden, around a bend in the road, a horde of enemy troops suddenly appeared on bicycles and Harley immediately opened fire with the machine gun. He sprayed the densely packed Japanese cyclists at close range, and claimed that those that were not killed outright abandoned their bikes and leapt into jungle. He reckoned that this engagement lasted barely five minutes.

Harley decided to remain on the road and wait in case any more of the enemy appeared, but when ominous noises suggested that the Japanese were trying to encircle their armoured vehicle, discretion became the better part of valour and he decided it was time to move off. Some distance down the road Harley and his crew came across the Argyles again, dug into a good defensive position on the far bank of the river. The AFV crossed the river just before the bridge was blown up and when they reached Lenngong Harley was able to give a full report to the Army commander of their actions. Within a short while Harley was ordered to hand over his AFV to the Argyles and he and his crew were hopeful that they would soon return to what he described as the 'ethereal element'.

By 18 December Harley was at a transit camp at Seletar, but when 62 Squadron was reformed on the 23rd he was back in Singapore at Tengah. By then most of its Blenheims had either been destroyed or were unserviceable and could not fly anyway. Among the first reinforcements to arrive was a force of fifteen Lockheed Hudsons which had been flown out to Singapore from Britain by volunteer crews from 53 Squadron. Wing Commander Lilly led the flight of Hudsons and many of the pilots, such as Flight Lieutenant O'Brian and Pilot Officer Robinson joined 62 Squadron.

Wing Commander McKern, the former CO of 100 Squadron, made a somewhat controversial decision to take over command of 62 Squadron because he had no previous experience of flying or operating Hudsons. Harley's role in the squadron at this point is unclear and there is nothing to suggest that he flew any sorties in the Hudson. Few reliable records exist for this period but it seems likely that Harley and other long standing officers from 62 Squadron were kept busy organizing the evacuation of Singapore and the move to Sumatra.

Harley remained with 62 Squadron at Tengah until 30 December when the squadron moved to Kluang, an airfield sixty miles up country in Malaya. On 7 January he was with the unit when it returned to Tengah, but on the 22nd it was given orders to evacuate its aircraft and personnel to Sumatra because Singapore was getting too congested. The evacuation of personnel was carried out by ship and 62 Squadron continued to operate as best it could from an airfield at Palembang with Hudsons and a small number of Blenheims.

It was probably 25 January, the last day that Harley was in Singapore, that his wife Pat managed to board a ship that was heading for her native country of Australia. They met very briefly and neither was certain whether they would ever see each other again but even after Pat boarded she realized that she was a long way from safety. The ship that was to sail before hers, and another behind, were torpedoed by a Japanese submarine and she could hear the screams of the passengers in the water. The captain announced over a loudspeaker that he could not stop or slow down to pick up survivors and the sounds of those drowning and thrashing about in the sea echoed in her ears for many hours.

Pongo Scarf's widow, Sallie, was one of many other nurses caught up in the evacuation and her departure was more complicated. At one point she embarked on the Blue Star liner *Empire Star* but later changed her mind and got off before it sailed. For many years Sallie felt guilty because she believed that the ship had been sunk on that voyage and she had let down the friends and colleagues who she had left on board.

The reality was that the 12,656-ton vessel had only been damaged by enemy action while off the coast of the Dutch East Indies. Sallie was pleased to discover the truth but the news was overshadowed by the fact the *Empire Star* was sunk eight months later on 23 October 1942.

Harley arrived in Palembang on 25 January and, as one of the most senior surviving officers, he was appointed as senior administrative officer working under Wing Commander McKern, the CO. The exact details of his operational role are not known but he later claimed that he flew a total of 200 hours in close support of the army and on night-flying sorties. From this time onwards it seems that his role was purely administrative and that he flew no more sorties.

There were two airfields on Sumatra that were used by the RAF and they were designated P1 and P2, the latter being approximately forty miles from Palembang. Most of 62 Squadron's aircraft and personnel were based at P2 where Wing Commander McKern made frantic efforts to camouflage the aircraft with brushwood, even going up in an aircraft to check that none could be see from the air. A number of 62 Squadron's aircraft were lost during this period and, on 1 January, Harley's former wireless operator, Flight Sergeant William Watson Martin (563352) was killed while flying with Flying Officer Haigh. Both Haigh's aircraft, L8441 and another 62 Squadron Blenheim, L1414, flown by Flight Lieutenant Lancaster, were shot down by Japanese fighters while they were attacking landing barges off the coast of Port Swettenham. Martin, who was 21 years old, had survived the experience with Harley of being stranded on the desert island but he could not escape the carnage of the Far East.

When Japanese parachute troops were dropped on the airfield at P1, from aircraft that were said to resemble Lockheed Hudsons, a bitter struggle ensued and although airmen and army units put up a good fight they could not hold it. The Japanese arrived in Sumatra and took the town of Palembang on 15 February, the same day as Singapore fell but, by then, most of 62 Squadron's personnel had moved south towards the port of Oesthaven. The ship carrying the main party departed on the 16th and arrived in Batavia, Java and most airmen were dispersed to a camp at Poerwakerta, while the aircraft were on the airfield at Semplek.

Harley arrived in Batavia on 16 February and was given command of a transit camp with the number KW III, but everyone knew that it was only a matter of time before the Japanese arrived.

In 1883, Batavia, the capital city of the Dutch East Indies had been badly affected when the volcanic island of Krakatoa had exploded. Fifty-nine years later in light of the Japanese advance and the mad panic to get away, it must have felt like a whirlwind had hit it.

At the transit camp individuals and parties were in Harley's own words, 'nominated' for evacuation by sea. That term is a very loose description of the process that took place, whereby airmen were told to form up in ranks for a roll call. If an airman was fortunate to hear his name called out, he then boarded a lorry that took him and others to the port of Tjilatap, where they embarked on ships that sailed for Ceylon or Australia.

There was not enough transport to get every serviceman down to the port but there were not enough ships to carry all those who were trying to escape from Java anyway. In the end, imprisonment, life and death were so much part of a lottery. Those whose names were not called were ordered to stand outside the building that acted as temporary headquarters and wait for the Japanese to arrive. Some were even told to smarten themselves up for it was feared that the enemy would not bother to take scruffy or dirty troops as prisoners of war. What part Harley played in this process we do not know but it could not have been easy for any officer to decide who should be left behind.

Leading Aircraftman James Graveson, a 23 year old from Maryport in Cumbria, was one of those left behind in Buitenzorg, Java and he later became one of the 549 British and Dutch prisoners (427 Allied and 122 Dutch) that died aboard the 6,400-ton *Suez Maru*. Thirty two year old Warrant Official Claude Henry Bere, 24 year old Corporal John Walter Steadman, LAC Donald Smith and Aircraftmen Vincent Thomas Shaw and Allan Noel Cliffe Walton were among the 62 Squadron personnel who had been captured in Java and died in the *Suez Maru*.

On 29 November 1943 the prison ship was torpedoed by the US Submarine *Bonefish* off the north coast of Bali and all 549 prisoners either drowned or were shot in the water because Japanese High Command dictated that POWs could not be allowed to escape. Typically the Japanese painted Red Crosses on those vessels carrying arms and ammunition but did not do so on those transporting prisoners of war and the captain of the *Bonefish* was unaware that there was human cargo on board. Remarkably, one prisoner lived to tell the tale because he was rescued some hours after the massacre by an Australian warship, HMAS *Ballarat*.

Aircraft of 62 Squadron continued to be lost right up to the point when Java was evacuated and on 24 February, Sergeants Allan Arthur Tearnan and Joseph Mercer were on board a Hudson that crashed in dense jungle on the island. Tearnan and Mercer decided to stick together but a third member of the crew went his own way and he was soon captured by the Japanese and taken as a POW. Tearnnan and Mercer were also captured but by local bandits who supported the Japanese and they were executed. The member of the crew taken prisoner by the Japanese is said to have survived the war.

Sallie Scarf had finally escaped the chaos and sailed from Singapore not long before the Japanese arrived, on a small Dutch tramp steamer, the 2,500-ton *Kota Gede*. She was accompanied by a small number of other nurses and staff from the hospital at Alor Star, including her friend Peggy Sale and Dr Peach, who had tried to save her husband. Typical of her good nature was the fact that she even adopted a dog, a bull terrier that had been abandoned by its owner and which she took with her on the ship.

After leaving Singapore however, the *Kota Gede* called in at Java to pick up stranded servicemen and it finally left there on 27 February bound for Ceylon. Those destined to sail on the *Kota Gede* had first to board the USS *Abberkirk* and many were disappointed when they were directed down a metal rung ladder on to the small steamer. There were a total of 2,000 servicemen on the ship including a large contingent of ground crew from 62 Squadron.

Harley escaped from Java on 2 March aboard the *Tung Song* a former RAF auxiliary vessel that had been known as the *Ann*. It was one of the last ships to leave. The remarkable thing was that he had to swim out to the ship to avoid capture because he had been left behind to carry out some last minute duties and the ship had already sailed. Fortunately he was a strong swimmer. It was typical of the service that, once he had managed to scramble on board the ship, everything and everybody had to be accounted for. Harley was made the officer in charge of the detachment and on 11 March, he wrote out a chitty to verify the number of servicemen on board:

Certified that a detachment of 77 officers and airmen when proceeding from Poerwokerto (Java) to Tjilitap for evacuation had no time to collect their kit and also that transport was not available for conveyance of baggage even if there had been time.

The undermentioned officer was one of the above detachment.

No	Rank	Name
37903	S/Ldr	Boxall

The *Tung Song* arrived in Fremantle on 13 March and, as the ship approached the safety of the Swan River, Harley may well have pondered over the fate of his colleagues. This period may certainly have been one for reflecting on recent events and, although Harley was probably not immediately aware of it, his close association with 62 Squadron had ended.

62 Squadron was eventually reformed at Akyab in Burma during February 1942, where the unit merged with the remnants of 139 Squadron and it was officially re-equipped with the Lockheed Hudson. In July 1943, 62 Squadron took on a new role when it was equipped with Dakotas and it was involved in supply dropping operations supporting the 14th Army. After being evacuated from Java however, most of the original personnel had been replaced and only a small number of those who had served at Alor Star were left.

By March 1942 over 7,000 RAF servicemen were listed as missing and many were never heard from again. Those that were evacuated or escaped capture and execution were the very lucky ones. During the course of the war 62 Squadron lost a total of 140 aircrew and ground crew and seventy-five of those are listed on the Singapore Memorial, which means that they have no known graves.

Seven of the 140, including the body of Squadron Leader Arthur 'Pongo' Scarf, are buried in Taiping War cemetery in Malayasia, while the rest are scattered around another sixteen cemeteries in Burma, India, Thailand, Malaysia, Israel and Japan. That fact alone shows the countries and theatres where 62 Squadron operated and the single airman buried in Yokohama Cemetery was a prisoner of war.

After arriving in Australia Harley faced an uncertain future, but before he could do anything about that, he had other more immediate and personal problems to worry about. When he landed in Fremantle, he made enquiries about his wife Pat and, having heard that she had arrived safely a few days earlier, he then had to find his way to her family home in Perth. He got a taxi from the port at Fremantle to Perth where, after making more enquiries, he eventually found the house. There was an emotional reunion.

Pat was totally overwhelmed because she had not heard anything of Harley since they had said their goodbyes at the quayside in Singapore nearly three weeks earlier. She feared that he had been captured or executed and was very much relieved to see him. Harley remained in Australia until early April. Much of the time that he spent there was with Pat and her family, but not all of it and Harley was kept busy with various matters that took him to several other Australian cities.

During his time in Australia Harley did a considerable amount of travelling but it is not know whether this was on RAF business or pleasure, although the former is much more likely. By 30 March he was in Melbourne where he stayed for six days, before leaving for Adelaide, where he remained for a further two days. On 9 April he finally left Australia aboard a troop ship that sailed for Colombo in Ceylon, on a dangerous voyage that was to last for eight days.

Harley remained in Ceylon until 16 May when he sailed aboard a troop ship for Bombay and during the four-day voyage he again acted as officer commanding the service personnel on board.

After landing in India Harley was sent to AHQ in New Delhi where he was briefed for his new position. He had been posted to RAF Jodhpur, where he was to take up a new appointment, a challenging role that would test his resolve and organizational skills in commanding a large RAF station.

CHAPTER 2

RAF Jodhpur

On 28 May 1942 the first entry in the Operational Record Book of RAF Jodhpur announced the arrival of Squadron Leader Boxall who had been posted to No. 2 Elementary Flight Training School on 9 April. Arriving a month later than planned, Harley was appointed as the CO of RAF Jodhpur. To begin with he had just two other officers to help him and Flight Lieutenant L.W. Davies and Pilot Officer G.P. Wood were his deputies.

The RAF's presence in India went back to December 1915 when, in the days of the Royal Flying Corps, 31 Squadron had arrived in Bombay with the BE 2c. From 1929 to 1939 the RAF had just eight squadrons in India but up to the outbreak of the Second World War, many of its units were equipped with obsolete aircraft like the Hawker Audax and Westland Wapiti. After the Japanese invasion of Malaya and Burma there was an urgent need for more modern types of aircraft and the building of new airfields that could service and handle them. Jodhpur was amongst the first to fulfil this role.

Situated in north-west India, the state of Jodhpur represented an area of 35,066 square miles in the region of Rajputana, whose economy was based on agriculture, the main crops being millet and maze. Salt and sandstone were also found there and there were marble quarries at Makrana. The capital city of Jodhpur was situated approximately 250 miles south-west of Delhi. It had been founded in 1459, by the Rathore Clan and named after Rao Jodha, but then being ruled by a succession of Maharajahs. The most imposing feature of the city was the huge Mehrangarh Fort that towered thirty-six metres above the city.

In 1942 the Maharajah of Jodphur was Umaid Singh, who had ruled since 1918 and, likc his predecessors, he was a powerful man who was entitled to a 17-gun salute on occasions of state. The Maharajah and his family lived in the state palace where banquets, dances and parties were held regularly. The palace had been designed and built in 1905 by Sir Swinton Jacob, who was a British Army officer serving in the Royal Engineers.

Subsequently there were many connections between Jodhpur and Britain but in 1925, when the Maharajah had visited London, it had been misreported that he had four wives. This was not true and the law in Jodhpur permitted only monogamous marriages, so he was only legally entitled to one. The other women with him were probably his daughters and the report could clearly have caused a lot of embarrassment and seriously affected diplomatic ties. Despite the blunder in the press the Maharajah was still very fond of the British and he and Harley were to become very good friends.

Harley's wife Pat arrived in Jodhpur shortly after her husband and she was to become a good friend of the Maharajah's daughter, Baiji, whose full title was Her Highness Shobogh Kaanwar Baiji Singh. Baiji had been educated in Britain, where she gained an air of independence and she was a very accomplished young woman. The two women spent a lot of time together and it seems that Pat was fascinated by the Indian way of life and fashion. Photographs taken at the time show Pat dressed in Baiji's saris on the balcony of her house in Jodhpur and they had a great deal of fun together.

On Thursday 9 July 1942 the Duke of Gloucester visited Jodhpur to celebrate the opening of the RAF station and more importantly to promote relations between the British, the Indian authorities and State Government. There was an official state banquet hosted by the Maharajah at what was referred to as Jodhpur Airport and there was no mention of RAF Jodhpur

Invitations were sent out by Lieutenant Colonel D.M. Field, who was the British Chief Minister in the Government of Jodhpur and, as might be expected, there was a strict dress code. Military officers had to wear best dress uniform while civilians wore tropical suits. The dress code for Indian gentlemen was the strictest of all and demanded that they should wear white achkans with saffron coloured safas or pagries, white breeches or chooridar pajamas and black leather shoes.

The banquet began at 1100 and a seating plan that has survived the ravages of time shows that His Royal Highness The Duke of Gloucester was seated exactly in the middle of the table, opposite His Highness the Maharajah of Jodhpur, who also held the rank of a group captain in the Indian Air Force. The Chief Minister, Lieutenant Colonel Field, was seated on the immediate left of the Duke, opposite Lieutenant Colonel Howard Kerr. Harley, being a humble squadron leader, was placed second from the end on the same side as the Maharajah, between a Major Allington and Captain Haj Singh. The most senior RAF officer present was Air Commodore T.M. Williams and he was seated on the immediate left of the Maharajah, directly opposite the Duke.

After the official visit the hard work of getting RAF Jodhpur operational began in earnest and among the first things that Harley had to do was establish a station headquarters. He also had to set up a Staging Post and a maintenance unit, 317 MU, that would be capable of storing a minimum of fifty aircraft, an assortment of light bombers and fighters that had to be made serviceable for issue to service units. The first personnel arrived at Jodhpur on 17 July when twenty airmen were detached for duty at the Staging Post from 301 MU in Karachi, while others were re-attached from No. 2 EFTS

As had been the case when Harley had commanded the airfield at Alor Star in Malaya, the security of the airfield at Jodhpur and its installations was a major concern. On 6 August a conference was held between Harley, the Commandant of the Jodhpur State Forces and the Inspector General of the Police and agreement was reached in several key areas.

(1) Jodhpur State Forces would provide three NCOs and eighteen IOR (Indian Other Ranks) for duties on the airfield at the main gate, SHQ, the armoury and any aircraft that needed guarding. Three NCOs and fifteen IORs would be provided for duties in the Technical Areas when required.

(2) Jodhpur Civil Police would provide one senior NCO and six IOR for duties in the domestic area. Guards would also be provided for the United States Army Air Corps Telegraphy Unit, a civil

wireless transmitting station and a D/F station.

Within a week of these arrangements being made the security situation had deteriorated to such an extent that the airfield guard had to be doubled and included an NCO and three airmen from the RAF. The trouble was mainly caused by calls for a separate Muslim state to be called Pakistan and Harley's first few months in India proved to be quite eventful, with personnel at RAF Jodhpur taking the brunt of bad feelings against the British. There were not only those who wanted a separate Muslim state but other Indians who demanded independence from Britain.

A meeting was held between Harley and Sir Donald M. Field on 11 August to discuss the ongoing political emergency. The Chief Minister was of the opinion that although there was the possibility of further trouble in the city, there would be no further disturbances against RAF Jodhpur. All RAF personnel had been warned to keep out of the city, especially after dark, for their own safety.

After the meeting Harley travelled to Delhi to report to senior officers at AHQ and he left the station under the command of Squadron Leader Bishop, AFC from No. 2 EFTS. He returned to Jodhpur the following morning and assumed command but by then the situation had stabilized because of the arrival of extra troops.

There was a lot of Chinese activity at Jodhpur, where a lot of aircraft such as the P66 Vultee Vanguard were being flown in and serviced by the Americans, prior to them being delivered to the Chinese Air Force. The Vanguard, powered by a 1,200 Pratt & Whitney engine was a single-seat fighter with an unusual feature in the form of rearward firing machine guns, aimed by the pilot with the aid of mirrors. The novelty was later removed.

The Chinese were also involved in the establishment of a wireless telegraphy station at Jodhpur and, in September, Harley met David Hsjung, a representative for Chinese Aeronautical Affairs. They discussed the arrangements for its operations and proposals that had been submitted to 226 Group HQ by Colonel Wai Cyiao Loo from the Chinese Air Force HQ in Karachi. There were already a number of other W/T stations at Jodhpur including an American unit and it had recently been proposed that those representing the civil authorities, the RAF and the USAAC should merge their facilities.

Harley also had to discuss the implementation of the Armed Forces (Special Powers) Ordinance Act with the Chief Minister for Jodhpur State, but on the first occasion of their meeting the Minister was unable to confirm whether it had been ratified by the Government of Jodhpur. One outcome of their meeting was that they agreed a plot of ground could be reserved for Christian burial for members of the Allied armed forces. The first two burials had already taken place and 1125411 Sergeant Roland Greaney was the first RAF casualty to be interred in what was known as plot R1. He had died on 2 July and his body was later reburied in the Delhi War Cemetery.

On 9 September Harley wrote to 226 Group Headquarters to inform the staff about the shortage of essential ground equipment at RAF Jodhpur and he made it clear in his letter that the only technical equipment available was a Rotol airscrew and a wheel extractor suitable for the Hurricane. The situation was so serious that a foot pump had to be borrowed from Burma-Shell and lifting blocks and trestles made from railway sleepers, that were taken from Jodhpur railway workshops. There were only twelve spark plugs suitable for the Roll-Royce Merlin engine and others were urgently required for Mercury, Cyclone and Twin Wasp engines.

At the same time Harley was pondering over the dispersal and concealment of aircraft again and he took the opportunity to discuss the matter with Wing Commander Fenwick when he passed through Jodhpur. What he proposed was to build a road from the perimeter track to the base of a 200 feet high hill, known locally as Chitter Hill. It was suggested that aircraft pens would be built on a site below the hill and Harley discussed his idea with public works, who required more detailed plans. However he was assured that there would be no objections on political grounds.

At the end of September 1942 Harley received a memorandum from the AOC India, Air Vice-Marshal Wigg. Its contents were meant to clear up any confusion about the division of responsibilities between 226 and 227 Group. If Harley had any doubts about his role and responsibilities before he read the memorandum, he would have had a lot more afterwards because the communication was contradictory and full of bureaucratic language.

The AVM pointed out to Harley that RAF Jodhpur had not yet officially been formed and although there was a nucleus of personnel stationed there, the term, 'RAF Jodhpur' was only being used to differentiate between the station and No. 2 EFTS. The AVM said that the nucleus of personnel at Jodhpur came under the command of 226 Group for all purposes except medical care. The station itself and No. 2 EFTS were under the command of 225 Group but all development work on the airfield was the responsibility of Wing Commander Martin at AHQ.

Despite the fact that Harley had been appointed as Officer Commanding RAF Jodhpur, Air Vice-Marshal Wigg seemingly attempted to redefine his role. He pointed out that Harley was only responsible for some public works, flying control, flying discipline, medical matters, rations and accommodation. On matters of camp discipline he could exercise the powers of officer commanding but each of the groups could exercise its own powers and deal with its own internal affairs as it wished. We do not know the rationale behind the AVM's memorandum but it is possible that Harley was being put in his place after complaining about the shortage of equipment.

Harley had little time for flying but, on 20 October, he took to the air in a civil registered Tiger Moth, VT-APS. With Squadron Leader Bishop as his passenger, Harley made two circuits and landings in what was possibly his first flight since early February.

The following day Harley signed a declaration in his new Air Force (India) Form 414, Pilot's Flying Log Book, which he noted as being his third and subsequently marked as No. 3:

> Certified that log books Nos 1 and 2 lost due to enemy action in Java. To the best of my knowledge and belief totals brought forward are correct as they appeared in my previous log.

The total hours flown as first pilot were logged as 600 by day but, rather surprisingly, only 35 by night

On 21 November Harley was occupied in checking out a number of landing grounds and he took-off from Jodhpur at 0950 with Captain Gerrard on board. They landed at Bhawi and then took-off again for Mathania which they inspected before returning to Jodhpur where they touched down at 1430. Over the following week Harley made another six flights with Captain Gerrard and inspected a number of landing grounds including those at Deesa and Bhuj.

The declaration announcing the official formation of RAF Jodhpur was eventually made on 27 November 1942, some six months after Harley had arrived there and it was confirmed by 'Official Formation Order Number 279'. The order stated that the formation of RAF Jodhpur would include station headquarters and 319 Maintenance Unit. The Staging Post (Number 46) and Salvage Section (Number 141) would remain as independent units. RAF Jodhpur was established as part of India 208 Establishment and under the control of 226 Group.

Harley carried out an aerial inspection of the airfield at Jodhpur on 2 December from a Tiger Moth accompanied by Mr Karanja of the Works Department. Soon after the formation order was issued Jodhpur became more active and three Hudson Mk.VIs arrived from Karachi to be put in storage. The airfield was designated priority 'B' status and both Nos. 2 and 3 Elementary Flying Training Schools were based there, along with No. 5 Meteorological Forecast Centre.

A variety of different aircraft passed through Jodhpur on any single day and among the civil types used for training and communication duties were Tiger Moths, Puss Moths and the DH Dragonfly. Of the distinct military types Bristol Blenheims, Avro Ansons, Hawker Hurricanes and Lockheed Hudsons were regular visitors, while transport aircraft like the Douglas DC2 and DC3 were amongst the larger variety. Most of these aircraft were transiting through Jodhpur from west to east and typically arrived from Karachi and departed for Delhi. The majority of the smaller types had been transported to India by sea, where they had been assembled before being flown to maintenance units where other equipment was fitted and modifications made.

Harley left Jodhpur on 15 December for a conference in Delhi attended by senior officers from AHQ. He flew in a Hudson piloted by Flight Sergeant Swann and returned on the morning of the 17th. The final movement before Christmas 1942 was the arrival of Blenheim V6629 from Allahabad which departed for Karachi at 1455.

For many airmen at RAF Jodhpur 1943 began with an impressive Station Commander's Parade that was held on Saturday 2 January. All officers from SHQ and 319 MU that were not on duty were ordered to attend and one of the four flights that made up the parade was of airmen from the newly formed RAF Regiment. The colour was hoisted at 0830 before the flights marched past the standard and Harley proudly took the salute.

Harley had to deal with a number of incidents on the airfield in the New Year and during the afternoon of 4 January a Lockheed Hudson, FK485, arrived escorting four Vultee Vengences, AN955, AN963, AN980, and AN907 but unfortunately the latter crashed on landing and the aircraft turned over and caught fire. The two crew were trapped inside the fuselage, but a crash crew arrived to rescue them and the pilot, Sergeant Hetherington and wireless operator/air gunner Sergeant Hagg escaped serious injuries. They were taken to Windham Hospital and a salvage team eventually cleared the runway so that the airfield could reopen again at 1830.

There were a number of particular problems associated with the Vengeance and on 7 January Harley met a representative from the Vultee Aircraft Corporation to discuss how they might be resolved. Three of them had force landed at Guadalpura on 23 December and it was decided that the representative should inspect the aircraft to ascertain whether or not they could be recovered and how. With the help of the Vultee representative the aircraft were eventually repaired and flown to Jodhpur, where they were overhauled by 319 MU.

From mid-January Harley's name rarely appears in the ORB although his log book shows that he was still active and he carried out another aerial inspection of the aerodrome on 16 January. On 7 February he was airborne in an Anson undergoing flying practice with Flying Officer Thomas. However his time at Jodhpur was drawing to a close. On 9 March he was promoted to the rank of acting wing commander and the last official function that he carried out in his role as officer commanding, took place on 31 March.

It was a ceremonial parade to mark the 10th anniversary of the Indian Air Force that had been formed on 1 April 1933 at Drigh Road Karachi with just five pilots. The guest of honour was the Maharajah of Jodhpur and he inspected the parade at 0900 before taking the salute with Harley. It was a sad occasion for Harley but he and his wife were to maintain their friendship with the Maharajah and his family for many years. The Maharajah and his daughter would continue to be an important influence in their lives and several years later they would become godparents to Harley's daughter.

At some point in either late 1942 or early 1943 there was an assassination attempt upon the life of the Maharajah but the details of what happened have never been released. It is believed that it took place while he was at the theatre, when a local dissident tried to shoot him was but overpowered and captured. Little is known of the fate of the would be assassin, but rumours circulated at the time, suggest that after being severely beaten during a short interrogation, he was summarily executed.

There is also something of a mystery surrounding Harley's last month at Jodhpur because after handing over command of the station he was posted to 319 Maintenance Unit based on the far side of the airfield. That was on 27 March but what his role was there is not known. He remained with the unit for just over a month before taking up his next challenging post.

Little is known of Harley's actions or movements during this time other than that he flew to Karachi on 16 April in a Hudson, accompanied by Flight Sergeant Swann, probably for a meeting concerning his next appointment at RAF Mauripur. The date that Harley was posted is not mentioned in his service record; it just notes 'South-East Asia Command'.

CHAPTER 3

RAF Mauripur and 229 Group

Harley took over command of RAF Mauripur from Wing Commander E.A. Keegan, his old friend from 62 Squadron, on 29 April 1943. Wing Commander Keegan's movements after the evacuation of Singapore are not known, but he had obviously been in India for some time and he had been given command of Mauripur in early April.

Mauripur was one of three RAF stations situated near Karachi, RAF Drigh Road being the closest of them to the city, situated on its southern boundary. There was also a seaplane base on the coast at Korangi Creek where the Catalinas of 191 and 212 Squadron were based. RAF Mauripur lay just over six miles north of Karachi and was to become an important airfield because, on 25 March 1943, only the month before Harley took over command of Mauripur, Transport Command had been formed.

Number 48 Staging Post RAF Mauripur soon became an airfield that was a vital facility for aircraft that were destined for the Far East and beyond, especially those that were operated by 179 Wing, the Transport Command parent unit in India. Many flights involved the transportation of troops to Burma and so the station ultimately came under the control of South-East Asia Command. It was planned that it should fulfil all its requirements for the various types of aircraft and cargos that were destined for stations further down the route towards the front line.

21 Ferry Control Unit was another important unit that was based at Mauripur. It received all the aircraft that were destined for the

RAF's India Command and was responsible for ferrying them to all the airfields in the Mauripur Sector. The Main Ferry Crew Pool was another unit based at Jodhpur and was the parent unit of all ferry crews serving in India, but it came under the overall command of 179 Wing. 317 MU had recently been transferred to Mauripur from Jodhpur and its role was to service, test and carry out major inspections of all types of aircraft.

There were several important issues to be resolved when Harley arrived at Mauripur and one of them again concerned the Vultee Vengeance and the fact that there was a shortage of pilots available who were trained to fly it. Some pilots from 21 Ferry Control had already received some training on the Harvard, with the aim of converting them to the Vengeance. The Main Ferry Crew Pool had only recently been transferred from Drigh Road and the move had caused a backlog of work and delays.

On 14 May Harley attended the first of a series of weekly meetings that were held in his room at station headquarters and a number of incidents had made sure that the issue of security was high on the agenda. There was a possibility that there was a saboteur at large on the airfield because only a few days before a Wellington bomber had mysteriously caught fire while parked at its dispersal. Despite the frantic efforts of a number of airmen who were immediately on the scene and that of the crash fire crew, who arrived within four minutes, the aircraft was completely burned out.

A few days later there was another serious fire that mysteriously broke out at a W/T Transmitter Station while the generator was being refuelled. Personnel were immediately on hand again to prevent the fire from spreading into the interior of the station but considerable damage was done before it was put out. The circumstances surrounding both these incidents were considered to be suspicious and Courts of Inquiry were convened to investigate.

It was on 9 June that Harley finally qualified for the substantive rank of squadron leader, some eight months after being appointed acting in the same rank and, although he still only held the rank of acting wing commander, by comparison to those who served in the RAFVR. in Britain, he had done quite well to rise from the rank of flight lieutenant in such a short time.

On 2 July Harley escorted Air Commodore Isles and Group Captain Chesfield on an inspection of 317 MU where they discussed improvements that could be made to the MT Section and transit aircrew facilities. The Air Commodore was of the opinion that there was too much waste in the MT system and he wanted to introduce a scheme that provided ongoing training for the rising population of 'floating' aircrew, so that they would be kept up to date and busy. The inspection was interrupted when a Bristol Beaufort crashed on take-off bursting into flames and although the aircraft was completely burnt out both members of the crew managed to escape unharmed.

August was a bad moth for accidents and, on the 8th, a Harvard and a Hurricane both made forced landings on the airfield. The following day another Hurricane made a forced landing between Malavi and Khamshet and the search party experienced a great deal of difficulty in reaching the crash site. When they did, they found the aircraft completely burnt out, it having seemingly exploded on impact. The aircraft had been carrying long-range fuel tanks and a subsequent Court of Inquiry, in which Harley was involved, came to the conclusion that the long-range fuel tanks had caused the aircraft to explode. It was recommended that in future only overload tanks that could be jettisoned in an emergency should be fitted to aircraft that were being ferried.

On 10 August a Bristol Bisley (Bristol Blenheim V) that was being flown by a Yugoslavian pilot in formation with a number of other aircraft, suddenly lost height and ditched in the sea. There were a number of eyewitness accounts of this incident including those of Harley and Flight Lieutenant Price who had watched events from a Dakota that was taking them on a staff visit to Jiwana. They were called as witnesses at the Court of Inquiry but the Operational Record Book does not give any further details.

A conference was held at Mauripur on 21 August to discuss the defence of the station and Squadron Leader James and Flight Lieutenant Miller represented 223 Group. It had previously been known as NORGROUP but, by 1943, it was a composite group that had been reformed from No. 1 Group (Indian) and was responsible for the administration of RAF units in north-west India.

Harley was informed about a scheme that involved training for 'backers up' – airmen and soldiers who would be used to defend Mauripur in case of an emergency. They also discussed the situation concerning some troops who were marooned at a wireless station on the Hongoli River and it was decided that an airdrop was the only way to get supplies to them. It was arranged for an Anson to carry out the operation and the next day bread, tins of corned beef and cigarettes were dropped within fifty yards of their position.

At the end of August Harley suddenly became ill and he was confined to his quarters, forcing him to hand over command on a temporary basis to Squadron Leader D.W. Law, who was the OC Training Flight. Harley was suffering from infective hepatitis and given twenty-one days' sick leave. This may well have been the beginning of the illness that was to plague him for many years and it was suspected that his experience on the desert island was to blame, particularly the fact that he had had to drink large amounts of dirty water to survive.

On 15 September there was a colour hoisting parade to celebrate the Battle of Britain and the records note that it was attended by the Station Commander. Despite his recent illness Harley would not have wanted to miss such an important occasion, because the Battle of Britain was still very much in the minds of all who served in the RAF

A very important guest of honour, Lord Louis Mountbatten, landed at RAF Mauripur on 6 October. In April 1942 had been appointed as Chief of Combined Operations and only the week before, as the Supreme Commander of the newly formed South-East Asia Command. The aircraft he arrived in was a specially prepared Avro York, serial number MW102 that had been built at Ringway Airport Manchester. It had been handed over to 511 Squadron at Lyneham in December 1943 before transferred to the strength of South-East Asia Command.

To make sure that everything went according to plan, Air Commodore D'Arcy Power had arrived the day before and met Harley to discuss arrangements for the visit. When Lord Mountbatten and his wife stepped off the aircraft at 2030 they were met by Air Vice-Marshal Baker from AHQ in Delhi and a number of other senior staff officers. As a mere wing commander Harley did not rank high enough to be on the list of officers who were introduced to Lord Mountbatten.

The following day as Lord Mountbatten's York was getting ready to depart, a Beaufighter, serial number X8228, swung off the runway and caught fire. Fortunately the pilot, Sergeant Rice, was not injured but the wreckage blocked the runway for a while and it may have been an embarrassing incident for Harley to deal with. However by the time that Lord Mountbatten's aircraft took-off at 0900 hours, the wreckage had been cleared away.

Many of the operational units that were destined for the Far East passed through Mauripur and, on 23 October, 89 Squadron arrived on its way to Ceylon from where it was to carry out intruder operations with its Beaufighter Mk. VI over Burma. The Dakotas of 117 Squadron also transited through Mauripur a week later and, having been formed at Khartoum in 1941 as a communications squadron, they were destined to remain in India for the rest of the war.

From October 1943 many of the aircraft that were loaned to Britain under the Lend-Lease Agreement from America, were flown directly into theatre, rather than being flown to the UK and on to their destinations in the Far East. These included many of the heavy bombers like the Consolidated Liberators that were to equip a number of RAF units in India for the forthcoming offensive in Burma and Siam.

Not all the crews who arrived in India were given the welcome that they thought they deserved and former Flying Officer Jim Gardner, who flew a Bristol Beaufort from England recalled his experience. His was one of two crews that flew brand new Beauforts from Filton to Mauripur on an epic journey that lasted three weeks. When they finally arrived an officer appeared to inspect the aircraft and looked disgusted at what he saw.

'What the hell are these?' he snidely asked.

'Bristol Beauforts sir,' replied Jim.

'Well you can take them back where you got them. We asked for Beaufighters.'

With so many different types of aircraft arriving and departing it was inevitable that accidents would happen, but it was rather amazing that the first fatality to occur on the airfield did not take place until 7 November. The aircraft, a Mosquito, LR465, had been carrying out an air test but crashed on landing and immediately caught fire, trapping the two-man crew. Eventually the navigator, Pilot Officer Stevens was pulled free but the pilot, Flight Lieutenant Van Riel remained trapped. There were a number of heroic attempts to free him and Flight Sergeant Norman, who was in charge of the rescue party, was so badly burned he later died of his injuries. Flight Lieutenant Van Riel was eventually released but it was too late to save him and he died soon after he was pulled from the wreckage.

Thirty-three year old Flight Lieutenant Zeger Van Riel had been awarded the Distinguished Flying Cross for his actions while flying Spitfires with 317 Squadron. He was buried in Karachi cemetery but after the war, his body was repatriated to his native country, Belgium.

Probably as a result of the number of accidents that had already happened, on 20 November a Flying Accidents Committee was set up and Harley became the chairman. Other members included Squadron Leader Prescott, Squadron Leader Price and Squadron Leader Manning. A week later the committee held its first investigation when a Lockheed Hudson of the Allahabad Flight, serial number FK642, crashed at Gurgoen, while en route from Mauripur to Allahabad.

This was the most serious accident to date; six officers and a single senior NCO being killed. The most senior officer was Wing Commander Hughes, who was the CO of 354 Squadron based at Cuttack which was to be equipped with the Consolidated Liberator bomber in November. The only two officers to survive were Pilot Officer Beadman of the Main Ferry Pool and Pilot Officer Roames from 224 Group. Both however were very badly injured.

At the end of 1943 Harley posted a report to AHQ with details of the pilots who had undergone training on Mauripur's Training Flight and there was a significant rise from the previous numbers. Fifteen pilots had completed refresher courses and twenty-nine had completed various conversion courses. A total of 102 hours of cockpit drill had been carried out and fifteen wireless operator/air gunners had been re-trained.

In December Harley was also able to report that over 300 aircraft had been turned around at RAF Mauripur including eighty-six from the newly formed Transport Command. Forty-eight civil aircraft had also been handled and there were over 300 movements by aircraft from 21 Ferry Control.

In early January 1944 Harley welcomed the Rajah of Faridkot to Mauripur to review the Airfield Guard Troop of the 43rd Garrison Company that had been raised in the State of Mauripur. The weather did not provide ideal for such an occasion and there were violent storms with three-quarters of an inch of rain falling in a very short time. The airfield was flooded but the rain was badly needed even though the water from the storm still only left the reservoirs one-third full.

On 14 January Harley received a secret report from the United States Army Air Corps claiming that a Japanese Zero fighter had been spotted in the area by one of its observers. As the nearest Japanese forces were many hundred of miles away in Burma it seemed unlikely that the aircraft was a land based machine but there remained the possibility that it could have been a carrier-borne fighter. In view of the definite nature of the report a flight of three Spitfires and a single Hurricane were armed and prepared in an immediate state of readiness. Two days later it was discovered that the sighting was almost certainly a false alarm when the 'Japanese' aircraft was spotted again and positively identified as an American built Vultee Vengeance.

Harley was ordered to report to Delhi for a briefing on 24 January and, as usual, left his deputy Squadron Leader Price in command during his absence. Later that day the Squadron Leader was at the controls of a Dakota when it overshot on landing and crashed into a drain on the airfield boundary. There had been a lot of rain the previous day and the runway was very wet, but also the 'Landing T' was facing the wrong way around, to indicate that the wrong runway was in use. Despite the mitigating circumstances Squadron Leader Price must have been embarrassed by the incident, especially as he was acting CO at the time. Harley returned to Mauripur on the 29th.

His time at the station was nearly at an end.

On 7 February Group Captain Toogood was posted to Mauripur from Allahabad and took over command of the station from Harley with almost immediate effect. Harley was posted to 229 Group HQ in Delhi to take up his position as Wing Commander Org. 1, 229 Group, the group having been formed on 12 December 1943. This new group took over the responsibilities of 179 Wing which had, in effect, been upgraded to group status. It was to carry out the same functions in India as 46 and 47 Groups within Transport Command in Britain. Harley was given ten days' leave and on the 13th he left Mauripur, flying in a Douglas DC 2 to Jodhpur and then on to Delhi.

He officially arrived at 229 Group HQ on 17 February 1944 but on that day he flew to Bombay and remained there for two days before returning to Delhi via Agra. Because of the nature of his role, the purpose of this flight and many others is not known and it is hard to distinguish any individual actions or decisions that he made while he was at 229 Group HQ. As the senior organizing officer in 229 Group he was responsible for organizing and authorizing everything to do with the safe passage of aircraft in its area of responsibility. We can also assume that he was happy in his work because, just two months after taking up the post, he made an application for a permanent commission. It was made just two days after Harley had been awarded the 1939/43 Star on 8 April:

From: Wing Commander C.H. Boxall (37903) RAFO.,
H.Q. 229 Group.
To: Air Officer Commanding H.Q. 229 Group, RAF
Date: 10 April 1944

Sir,

Application For Appointment to a Permanent Commission in the Royal Air Force – A.M.O.A188/1944

I have the honour to request that I may be considered for appointment to a Permanent Commission in the Royal Air Force under the terms of A.M.O. A.188/1944.

2. I attach herewith completed proformae, in triplicate,

as set out in the Appendix to the above quoted Air Ministry Order.

3. Although I am nearly twelve months above the age for normal application, I request that my case be considered under the second sentence of para. 4 of the above quoted Air Ministry Order.

4. I may add that in 1939, I was provisionally selected for a Permanent Commission without the necessity of passing the normal examination but, on the outbreak of the European War, all grants of Permanent Commissions were suspended. I have the honour to be, Sir, Your Obedient Servant.

The appendix to Harley's application contained precise details of his service history from 11 May 1936, the day he had joined the RAF. What might have brought back bitter memories was that he had to detail the incident in April 1940 when he had force landed on the desert island. He had to admit that he had received a severe reprimand from the AOC and it might have seemed that it could never be forgotten and it came back to haunt him on a regular basis.

There was one slight discrepancy in Harley's record and he noted that he had been awarded his flying badge in November 1936, when it was actually in October that year. It was not a major error but he was effectively cheating himself out of a month's seniority.

Harley's new appointment at 229 Group meant that he would need to do a lot of flying on communications duties because he would regularly have to visit outlying staging posts and landing grounds. Even though he had recently flown aircraft like the Hudson and Dakota his actual flying experience from November 1942 to April 1944 amounted to less than 49 flying hours.

There was the obvious need for Harley to undertake some multi-engine flying training and during April made a number of flights in the Avro Anson. On the 10th he completed four circuits and landings with Flight Lieutenant Yendall and five days later they flew a low flying exercise together. Harley later completed another low flying sortie before flying Wing Commander Crawford and three other officers from Palam (Delhi) to Bairagrah on the 28th. By the end of the month the number of his total flying hours had risen to 987 hours and 55 minutes

This was an exciting but anxious time for Harley because his wife Pat was pregnant and was expecting the arrival of their first child by the end of June. They were living in New Delhi, which was a very hot and dusty place and especially uncomfortable for a woman in her condition. It had therefore been decided that for the last few months of her confinement she should go to live where it was cooler and was taken to Simla (now Shimla). Accessible by a sixty-eight mile long railway, Simla was a hill station in Kashmir, situated 7,000 feet above sea level, in the foothills of the eastern Himalayas.

In the days of the British Raj, for six months of the year, Simla had been the seat of Government, because the intense heat on the plains made working conditions uncomfortable. Described by Kipling as 'A little bit of England in India' it had then been a place where the British liked to hold garden parties and tennis parties. By 1944 that had all changed although Simla still had a very British ambience with an Anglian church and a general hospital where Pat gave birth to their first child, a girl, on 1 July. She and Harley decided to call her Sallie after Sallie Scarf, who had recently returned to India where they had all met up again.

By now Sallie had re-married. Her new husband was an army officer, Major Stewart Gunn and, as both couples were living in New Delhi, they were able to see each other regularly. For the sake of old times, it was decided that Sallie should be the godmother of baby Sallie, but instead of Major Gunn being named as the other godparent, it was agreed by all, that it would be more appropriate and fitting for the godfather to be named as Arthur Scarf.

Harley did not get a lot of time to socialize or to spend with his wife and daughter and during August he regularly flew to a number of those airfields and staging posts that were used by Transport Command. In the same Dakota, serial number KG724, he visited Dum Dum (Calcutta), Cuttack, Vizagapatam and St.Thomas Mount

(Madras).

On 26 August Harley flew an Armstrong Whitworth Ensign from Mauripur to Palam. The four-engine passenger transport was the largest aircraft ever built for Imperial Airways and only fourteen were ever produced. It has been claimed that the aircraft was under-powered and one former Imperial Airways flight engineer commented of the Ensign, '… it gave the best twin-engined performance of any four-engined aircraft that the company ever operated.' The Ensign that Harley flew was almost certainly G-ADST (Elsinore) that was on the strength of 24 Squadron. Very few RAF pilots would have had the privilege of flying such a large aircraft and even fewer got the opportunity to fly the Ensign.

One important job that Harley carried out involved him having to fly back to England, to carry out a route survey and making an assessment of Transport Command's staging posts en route to the UK. His survey began when he carried out an assessment of a number of staging posts in India on 29 October, flying a Dakota from Delhi to Bombay, then on to Bangalore before going on to Colombo in Ceylon. Apart from any RAF business he may have had in the country, Harley could have had another more personal reason for visiting Ceylon. His brother Duncan was serving there in the Royal Signal Corps and it is known that the two men did meet up there on several occasions.

Harley stayed in Ceylon until 2 November when he made the return journey but remained at Bangalore for two days, before proceeding to Bombay and Delhi. There he was briefed for the next stage of an epic journey that would take him to Europe and Britain. Although he returned to Mauripur before setting out, there is no mention of him flying back there from the details in his log book and it is possible he returned by train.

On 14 November 1944 Harley left Mauripur in an Avro York, MW109, and flew to Shibah in Iraq before continuing to Cairo the same day. In his log book he noted that during this flight he flew as second pilot and it seems that by now he had a considerable amount of experience on both the York and Dakota. He remained at Cairo until the 16th when he departed in a Dakota for Malta, again noting that he flew as second pilot. The following day Harley flew in the same Dakota to Elmas in Sardinia and after only a brief refuelling stop there, continued to Lyneham in Wiltshire, where he arrived on the evening of the 17th.

It must have been strange sensation to be back in England for the first time in over five years and one can only imagine how he felt after being out of the country for so long. He returned to a cold bleak land that was in so many ways different to the Far East and India where he had effectively made his home with his wife, Pat. What Harley's duties were when he arrived in England is not known but they almost certainly involved meetings and discussions with senior officers of 46 Groups and it is quite likely that his month-long visit must have included some leave and that he visited his father and family in Handsworth.

On 12 December Harley returned to India and the first leg of the journey involved a flight from Lyneham to Elmas in a Dakota, before proceeding on to Castel Benito and Cairo West the same day. The next day he flew on to Habbaniyah in Iraq with the same aircraft, where he remained overnight before continuing to Shibah. He finally arrived in Karachi on the 17th but immediately began another round of visits that involved flights to Jodhpur, Palam, Ratmalan (Ceylon) and Santa Cruz (Bombay).

By Christmas Harley must have been exhausted but in the New Year he continued his inspections, regularly flying and visiting staging posts in a Beechcraft Expeditor, that may have been amongst his favourite aircraft to fly. On New Year's Day 1945 Harley was Mentioned in Dispatches for his part in the operations and evacuations concerning 62 Squadron in 1942. By this time 62 Squadron was also based in India at Comilla and operating Dakotas on supply dropping operations to the 14th Army. Of those that had served with it in the Far East during 1939 very few of the original personnel remained

In February he was busy flying himself between Palam, Nagpur, Yelahanka and Mauripur, always in an Expeditor. His final flight that month was in the Armstrong Whitworth Ensign again on the 28th, when he flew from Palam, to his old command at Jodhpur and then back to Mauripur. By then Harley's time at 229 Group was nearly at an end and he was about to be posted to 108 Wing. At this point Harley's total flying hours were 1,177 hours 10 minutes.

CHAPTER 4

108 Wing

108 Wing was formed in Karachi and although its establishment was authorized by Formation Order 282 on 24 September 1944, the unit did not become operational until February 1945. It was a transport wing under the control of 229 Group in South-East Asia Command. The wing was initially under the command of Flight Lieutenant R.P. Timms but due to a shortage of officers and airmen its operational status under his control was limited.

Harley was promoted to the rank of acting group captain on 13 February and appointed as CO of 108 Wing with immediate effect. The move from New Delhi to Karachi meant that he and Pat had to leave old friends behind again but it was probably more difficult for Pat than for Harley, who had the daily care of their daughter to think about. Probably the worst thing for Pat was having to say farewell to Sallie, not long after they had just met up again.

The responsibilities of 108 Wing were set out in a directive from 229 Group dated 15 March 1945 and to begin with the headquarters were located in the Old Government Buildings in Karachi. Soon after Harley took over however, the army moved in and 108 Wing had to move to new premises called Oriental Buildings.

Traditionally a wing was made up of three squadrons but 108 Wing's main role was to provide organizational and administrative support for a number of transport squadrons that were carrying out a vital role in India.

Immediately after he had been appointed Harley called a conference with the wing's headquarters' staff to inform them about its operational role and their duties. He then held another conference with Wing Commander Woffenden to discuss preliminary plans for setting up signals facilities at Wing HQ. Two external landlines were required and seven internal extensions, as well as direct teleprinter connections to 229 Group HQ and the airfields at Drigh Road and Mauripur.

Other officers assigned to 108 Wing were Wing Commander A.J. Price who was appointed the senior administrative staff officer and Squadron Leader J. E. Glenny who was responsible for transport and ferry operations. Squadron Leader Hungerford was appointed the OC Traffic, while Flight Lieutenant J.P. Steel became the adjutant. Flight Lieutenant Timms remained with the wing and became the Intelligence Officer. The only aircraft that 108 Wing operated in its own right were two Beechcraft Expeditors and two Harvards that were used for communication duties.

On 1 May Harley visited his old station at Mauripur to meet the CO of the troop transit camp. Later the same day Harley held another meeting at Drigh Road to discuss the implications of using the airfield there as the entry point for trooping flights into India and what facilities it would need.

The majority of the trooping flights at this stage had originally been planned as part of Operation Dracula, that was an airborne and seaborne invasion of Japanese held positions around Rangoon in Burma. It had been proposed that other trooping flights from the UK to India should begin properly in July with an initial airlift of 3,500 troops. By October 1944 it was planned that a total of 17,500 troops were to have been flown to India and that meant a lot of organizing for Harley and 108 Wing. Many of the trooping flights terminated at Mauripur and personnel were then ferried further down country in the Halifaxes and Dakotas of 10, 76 and 77 Squadrons.

May was a very busy month and as Harley noted in the ORB, the small scale trooping scheme began with the Dakotas of 47 Group flying in troops from England. The first flights were carried out by 187 Squadron and they transported troops from Merryfield near Taunton, down the route to Poona, south-east of Bombay. The flights out to India involved nine refuelling stops and an average distance of 800 miles on each sector, between staging posts. Harley was able to report to 229 Group HQ that, during May under this scheme, a total of thirty-nine aircraft had arrived carrying 845 troops with the average passenger load per aircraft being twenty-two.

The Short Stirling was also engaged on trooping but was mainly used on transport flights and two of them were deployed flying the route between Karachi, Calcutta and the UK. In May the same two aircraft were used to fly some 12,000 lbs of spare parts to Ceylon, which were to be used to get another Stirling that had been stranded there, flying again. 229 Group HQ authorized the aircraft to be diverted to Ratmalana for this purpose and each Stirling carried 6,000 lbs of spares.

On 10 May Harley was at Mauripur when a BOAC Avro Lancastrian arrived, homeward bound on the first round trip route trial from Britain to Australia. The aircraft was a civilian airliner, based on the design of the Lancaster bomber and the type would enter service with RAF Transport Command the following year. The service that was jointly run between BOAC and Qantas began at the end of June and there was one flight a week in each direction. Flights to the UK passed through Mauripur on Thursdays while those to Australia departed on Saturdays.

On 5 June a conference was held at Wing HQ to discuss the organization and setting up of No. 202 Staging Post at Drigh Road, an issue that had been raised a few days earlier. It was agreed that the personnel of No. 8 Ferry Pool at Mauripur should be transferred to Drigh Road and they would form the nucleus of the staging post. At the same time it was agreed the ferry flight at Santa Cruz would be absorbed into No. 56 Staging Post and that was to be transferred under the control of 108 Wing.

Harley must have loved flying the many different types of aircraft that passed through Mauripur or Drigh Road and on 14 June he had another new experience when he flew a Sunderland flying boat for the first time. He flew it from Korangi Creek, Karachi to Jiwani, where he stayed overnight. He noted in his log book that the Sunderland belonged to BOAC and the aircraft was almost certainly one of six Mk. IIIs purchased by the company at the end of 1942. The aircraft had been modified so that they had a faster cruising speed than their RAF counterparts and the BOAC Sunderlands manly operated a mail service from Poole, to Nigeria and India. They could carry only seven passengers.

In the middle of June a Halifax from the Empire Air Navigation School arrived at Mauripur to carry out a liaison visit and the aircraft, that had been named *Capelia*, was fitted with the most modern navigation systems. During its two days stopover, Harley was one of many pilots and ground crew who looked around the Halifax. So keen were personnel to discover how everything worked that demonstrations were organized and the crew gave talks on the technical aspects of Gee and Loran.

At the end of the month there was another incident that could be connected to events that were to happen six months later, when Harley noted in the Wing's routine orders that there was widespread discontent about the quality of catering. The complaints had been made about the standard of food served in the messes of the transit camps at Mauripur, Palam and Juhu. The complaints were investigated by 108 Wing's catering officer, Flight Lieutenant Taylor, who found them all to be fully justified. Harley claimed that the problems had arisen because the catering contract had been handed over to another company and he admitted that it was unlikely the quality of food would improve in the near future. He said that until the standard of catering improved the only sanction that he could take was to impose fines on the caterers and hope things got better. Typical of Harley's role was that one day he would be dealing with problems concerning such issues as food and catering and then a short while later having to make decisions on serious technical and engineering matters.

In early July there were complaints from a technical officer at 56 Staging Post that outer the skin of propellers fitted to some Spitfire Mk. XIXs was peeling off when the aircraft encountered certain weather conditions, even so much as light rain. The reports were sent to 229 Group HQ and Harley sent Flight Lieutenant Parker, the 108 Wing ferry operations officer to Santa Cruz to see what could be done. It was eventually decided that all Spitfires fitted with the JCS type propeller should be grounded until other types arrived that could be fitted.

Between 14 and 31 July, 108 Wing was kept busy with Operation Zipper, an airlift that the RAF's Transport Command was carrying out on behalf of the army. It involved the sorting and forwarding of a total 161,246 lbs of freight to various destinations in India, but mainly to Bombay and Agra. Although most of the freight had arrived from areas outside the jurisdiction of 108 Wing it still bore the brunt of the responsibility for dealing with it, because most of it arrived at Mauripur. At the same time Harley complained that the wing had to deal with a backlog of passengers who had to be processed and then flown out to various other destinations.

The first batch of British prisoners of war from camps in Siam passed through Mauripur on 4 September on their way back to the UK. Harley received orders from 229 Group HQ that they were to be interrogated by the 108 Wing intelligence officer, Pilot Officer Kiders. He was instructed to find out as much as he could about each man's experiences and in particular the accounts of what had happened on the Burma – Siam Railway, known as the Death Railway.

It is interesting to note that the term 'Death Railway' was used at such an early stage and it indicates that the authorities were aware of what had been going on. The reports were dispatched to 229 Group HQ immediately. For those officers like Harley who had been in the Far East when the Japanese had attacked four years earlier, reading them they may well have been a harrowing experience.

In October Harley had to deal with the fact that many of the crews of 10, 76 and 77 Squadrons, who were by then flying the Dakota Mk. III and IV, had not completed the necessary number of training hours laid down by Transport Command. As a result Harley agreed with 229 Group to introduce a new lower standard but he ruled that in future only the most experienced crews should be used on trooping flights. Three flying instructors were posted in from Baroda to carry out training duties and one was attached to each squadron.

Harley was involved with the setting up of a new unit called 1558 Heavy Flight that was initially equipped with two Stirlings whose main role was to carry spare parts to RAF units in South-East Asia Command. These were the same two Stirlings that had flown spare parts to Ceylon in May but it was agreed with 229 Group that the unit's strength should be five aircraft. As a result it was arranged that three more Stirlings would be flown out from the UK as soon as possible.

On 5 December 1945 Harley received a letter (2011/D.S.D.) from the Air Ministry in London requesting details of 62 Squadron's operations in the period immediately after the Japanese had invaded Malaya and Singapore. Harley's response was set out in a four-page document dated 20 December, marked confidential and titled, Report on Malayan and N.E.I. Operations 1941/42. In the report Harley noted the names of those who had been reported missing, presumed killed, in operations and they included Flight Lieutenant Lancaster, Flying Officer Haigh, Sergeant Dawson and Sergeant Stafford. He also mentioned that Flying Officer Frostick had been wounded in action. Under the section 'Reports For Meritorious Service Other Than Immediate Awards Made At The Time', Harley wrote 'Nil'. That he did so might have surprised some people who suspected that he was responsible for recommending Squadron Leader Arthur Scarf for the Victoria Cross. However the only mention of Pongo in the report states that he, 'Died of wounds received in air action'.

For some years it was a mystery who recommended Pongo for the award and because he and Harley were very close friends, as were their wives, some people naturally assumed that it was he. It can be confirmed that Harley did not make the recommendation for Arthur Scarf to be awarded the Victoria Cross or any other medal, but the officer that did was another former 62 Squadron pilot.

In December 108 Wing operations were badly affected by adverse weather conditions that persisted between the UK and India that seriously limited the number of trooping flights. Also an order enforced by 47 Group issued on the 15th limited the number of passengers that could be carried in a Liberator to eighteen. They had up to that time carried twenty-one passengers and Harley estimated that would lower the number of passengers carried per month from 4,056 to 2,808. An additional problem was that 426 Squadron, that was based at Tempsford, was withdrawn from the trooping programme during the third week in December and disbanded. Together with other factors, such changes would have a great impact upon events in the New Year.

CHAPTER 5

Mutiny and Ill Health

Most of the official records for 108 Wing end very suddenly on 31 December 1945 and those elements that have survived in the National Archive have been heavily censored. That is because of the so-called 'mutiny' that took place at Drigh Road, Mauripur and other RAF stations in India and the Far East. The airmen who worked on 108 Wing were amongst the first to walk out and so presumably, as Harley was their Commanding Officer, he would have been very much involved.

Rather ironically the main reasons behind the Indian mutiny was demobilization, although bad food and conditions featured in both incidents. Another source of discontent according to Commander Geoff Pell, whose father was a flight sergeant at Mauripur, involved BOAC, which was re-establishing its trunk routes through India. RAF airmen were being used to service and maintain BOAC aircraft that passed through Mauripur and other RAF airfields. Commander Pell's father described it as being a 'red rag to a bull' because the airmen were getting less pay than their civilian counterparts for doing the same job. He claimed that whole groups of airmen downed tools, refused to obey orders and the atmosphere became very ugly.

According to former Flying Officer Malcolm Laidlay, who was one of the officers at the aircrew transit camp that is exactly what happened. One night he was returning from Karachi on his motor-bike and was passing the airmen's mess when he was attacked. Some airmen recognized the fact that he was an officer and rocks and stones were hurled in his direction and the crowd of mutinying airmen tried to block the road. Although he was hit, he was not hurt but he said facing a group of angry, menacing looking airmen was not an experience he would not want to repeat.

When Air Commodore Jarman, the AOC of 229 Group, visited Mauripur on 20 January a number of junior NCOs and airmen stopped work. Notices were put up in 108 Wing's cookhouse at Mauripur informing airmen about the action and urging others to be sympathetic and to join the strike. The matter was soon put into the hands of senior officers such as Air Marshal Keith Park, who addressed a mass meeting of airmen at Seletar in Singapore.

What Harley's role was during the dispute is not known but his log book proves that he was busy flying between Drigh Road, Jodhpur, Palam and Mauripur. On most occasions he carried a number of passengers and on 7 January in the middle of the crisis, he flew in Expeditor, HB255, carrying out some local flying with a Flight Lieutenant Bird. The following day however was obviously business and he flew Squadron Leader Barrier, Flight Lieutenants Butt, Warburton and Bird, from Drigh Road to Jodhpur, then on to Palam.

On the 10th he flew Wing Commander Horsfall, Squadron Leader Barrier, and Flight Lieutenants Butt and Bird from Palam to Jodhpur in the same Expeditor. The next day Harley flew the same four officers from Jodhpur to Drigh Road and that was the last flight that he made in the month of January. The purpose of the these flights is not known but the fact that a group captain, wing commander, a squadron leader, as well as several other officers, were going from one airfield to another, suggest that they were involved in trying to resolve the dispute.

At this point Harley's reoccurring illness began to cause him problems again and, on 28 January, it is noted in his Service Record that he was, 'non effective sick'. He was suddenly posted out from 108 Wing and on to the strength of the Headquarters British Air Forces South-East Asia Command. On 4 February he was sent to No. 10 General Hospital in Delhi, where he was diagnosed with tuberculosis and on the same day he was posted to RAF Bombay.

Harley's final flights took place on 6 and 7 February and they were to take him to another military hospital that came under the command of RAF Bombay. First of all he flew in Dakota KP624, with Flight Lieutenant Dewel from Mauripur to Santa Cruz. The following day he flew with Dewel again in the same aircraft to

Poona, approximately sixty miles south-east of Bombay. The final total in Harley's log book is 1,246 hours 45 minutes.

For six months Harley languished in the hospital being treated and assessed before a decision was made to transfer him to another better equipped and more specialized hospital. It was obvious that his time in the RAF was coming to and end and that because of his ill health and his age, his application for a permanent commission would be rejected. There was one saving grace however and in February Harley was informed by the Air Ministry that he would be allowed to retain his rank as acting group captain.

News of Harley's ill health and predicament soon reached the ears of senior officers and on 12 March 1946, the AOC 229 Group, Air Commodore Jarman wrote a testimonial on his behalf. The Air Commodore had spent much of the war with Bomber Command and he had been awarded the DFC while with 77 Squadron, and the DSO while serving with 76 Squadron. His testimonial gives the best description of any, of what Harley's role and responsibilities were with 229 Group and 108 Wing.

To Whom It May Concern

Testimonial

It affords me considerable satisfaction to be able to express my appreciation in this form of the sterling qualities of Group Captain C. H. Boxall, who is shortly to leave the service after a distinguished service career. The service is losing a first class officer in all respects. He possesses sound judgment, determination and the capacity for hard work being above the average

Group Captain Boxall served under my command for over ten months in the capacity of Group Captain commanding a wing in Karachi. He has been directly responsible for immediate control of all air trooping aircraft, which handle 10,000 passengers a month, all trunk route aircraft entering and leaving India and also scheduled airlines, both civil and military, passing through the Karachi area. He has also had under his control Air Transport Stations covering over one third of India, including four Dakota squadrons, and a Liberator squadron; also an Air Transport Training Unit. His command comprised ten stations and over 8,000 officers and men.

He has during his period of command, built up his organization to an extremely high pitch of efficiency by dogged perseverance and drive against most serious difficulties and set backs and it is a matter of extreme regret to me and a serious loss to the Service that he is, by reason of him being over the prescribed age limit, compelled to be demobilized after serving in the Royal Air Force for ten years.

I can confidently recommend that Group Captain Boxall can and will undertake with success any employment which calls for a good general knowledge, a particular knowledge of Air Transport operations and organization, loyalty, determination, tact and drive, and would like to take this opportunity of wishing him every success in whatever new employment he undertakes.

(G.T. Jarman)
Air Commodore
Air Officer Commanding
229 Group, RAF

There was also a second testimonial from Air Vice-Marshal Charles Edward Neville Guest, the senior air staff officer at South East Asia Command headquarters. What the AVM may or may not have been aware of was that he and Harley were old boys of the same school, King Edward VI, in Birmingham.

Because the AOC was thirteen years older than Harley there is no possibility that they had ever met at the school, but there was an Old Boys association. Former pupils were actively encouraged to join the Aston Edwardian Society that had been formed out of the Old Edwardian Rugby Football Club in 1889. Its aims were for pupils to maintain contact with the school and to encourage the use of its sporting facilities for games such as tennis and squash. If they were both members of the society then it is quite likely that they would have been aware of each other's backgrounds because of the lists that were published about those serving overseas and receiving awards.

Wing Commander Boxall has served under my command for

over two years and, as he is shortly leaving the Royal Air Force, I would like to place on record my appreciation of his loyalty and help during this period, with the hope that it may be of assistance to him when finding employment.

I can say without fear of contradiction by any who may know him or have served with him, that he is an outstanding officer who combines the qualities of leadership and a high standard of organizing ability with a thorough appreciation of man management. His various appointments as Officer Commanding Mauripur Air Station, Chief Organizing Officer in my Transport Group Headquarters and finally, Group Captain in command of the Transport (and Air Trooping) Wing at Karachi, indicates the confidence and trust that I had in him which he has repaid with unswerving loyalty and marked efficiency.

He was responsible with others for the organizing and implementing of Transport organization through India in wartime in the face of many difficulties, this during two hot seasons without any leave.

A quite reserved and popular officer, possessing determination and staying power which belied the outward appearance of a frail physique. I am confident that he can make a success of any task entrusted to him which requires hard work and organizing ability.

These views represent my personal opinion of this officer, and must not necessarily be taken as official views.

(C.E.N. Guest)

Air Vice-Marshal

The AVM went on to become the AOC of No. 1 Group, Bomber Command, Assistant Chief of the Air Staff (Operations) and he was later promoted to the rank of air marshal. After his retirement he also carried out a role that in different circumstances would have been ideally suited for Harley, when he became an advisor to BOAC and the Air Ministry on air safety.

During his time in hospital Harley had a lot of time to reflect upon the past and think about his old friends like Pongo Scarf, who had been dead for over four years and were seemingly forgotten. That was not the case however and probably unbeknown to Harley at the time, Group Captain Norman Irving had made a recommendation that Squadron Leader Arthur Scarf should be awarded a medal.

RECOMMENDATIONS FOR HONOURS AND AWARDS

Particulars of meritorious service which is made:

On 9th December 1941, all available Blenheim aircraft of Norgroup, comprising the remnants of 27 and 62 Squadrons, and a detachment of 34 Squadron, assembled at RAF Butterworth, were ordered to attack in daylight the advanced operational base of the fighter squadrons of the Japanese Air Force at Singora, Siam, which were supporting the landing of enemy forces. The aircraft taking part in the sortie were on the point of taking off when a combined dive-bombing and low machine-gun attack developed, damaging or destroying all the Blenheims with the exception of one, which had just become airborne a few seconds before the raid started. This aircraft was piloted by Squadron Leader A.S.K Scarf of No. 62 Squadron, with Sgt. Calder and Sgt. Rich as Navigator/Bomb Aimer and Wireless Operator/Air Gunner respectively.

Squadron Leader Scarf circled the airfield during the attack and witnessed the debacle. When it was over, it would have been entirely reasonable for him to have abandoned the projected operation which was intended to be a formation sortie, but he decided to press home on Singora with his single aircraft. He knew that this individual action could not inflict much material damage but he must have appreciated the moral effect his action would have on the remainder of the Squadron who were helplessly watching their aircraft burning on the ground. Those who knew this officer would realize that he could not have come to any other decision for he was a natural leader, eager to engage the enemy.

He completed his attack successfully in the face of severe opposition, which included attacks by a considerable number of enemy fighters, in the course of which he sustained mortal wounds. The enemy continued to engage him in a running fight which lasted practically to the Malayan border, and his crew testified to the brilliant evasive action he fought in his valiant attempt to return to his base. Owing to his wounds, however, he was unable to do so, but he accomplished a successful forced landing near Alor Star without injury to his crew. Although he was received into hospital, he died shortly after admission.

I suggest that outstanding act of gallantry and determination in the face of the enemy is deserving of the highest award.

State what recognition is recommended. VICTORIA CROSS (Posthumous).

Group Captain Irving submitted the recommendation on 18 March 1946 and it was supported by Group Captain R.G. Forbes who signed himself as being the Commanding Officer of NORGROUP. The AOC confirmed the award on 29 March noting very simply, 'I agree'. It would be several months before the recommendation was acted upon.

During the first week in June Harley was transferred by hospital ship from the military hospital in Bombay to a hospital at Robert Heights in Pretoria, South Africa. It was while he was there, undergoing extended treatment that he had time to reflect upon his life again and began to write his memoirs.

Leaving India was a depressing time for Harley, not least because of the circumstances of his departure, his illness and the sudden removal from a job that he loved. Over the years he had made many good friends, amongst them the Maharajah of Jodhpur with whom he had played polo on several occasions, despite the fact that he lacked the necessary equestrian skills.

Because of the close friendship between the Maharajah's daughter Baiji Singh and Harley's wife Pat, it had been decided that she should become the godmother of their daughter, Sallie, who was baptized on 22 January 1945. Because the service took place in New Delhi, Baiji was unable to attend but a proxy took her place and Baiji's full name, Shobagh Kanwar Baiji, was recorded as being Sallie's godmother on the baptismal certificate.

Baiji Singh was a beautiful woman who had an air of independence and she later changed her religion from Hindu to

Christian which was a very radical thing to do at the time and her decision no doubt angered her father, the Maharajah. There is little doubt that Baiji was a woman far ahead of her time.

Shortly after he arrived in South Africa Harley received a letter that had been forwarded to him via the Defence Headquarters in Pretoria. The letter was from the Malaya Reports Section in the Air Ministry in London and it concerned the observations of a former Sergeant T. Hayes who had served on 62 Squadron. Sergeant Hayes had already left the RAF but he had taken the trouble to write to the Air Ministry and report some air actions that he had seen during the Japanese invasion.

The letter from the Air Ministry requested that, if possible, Harley should confirm either or both of these incidents and asked if he was willing to recommend a posthumous Mentioned in Dispatches award in respect of the crews. Mr Hayes' letter had obviously been prompted by the news of the award of the Victoria Cross to Squadron Leader Scarf and it sounds from his description of events as though his duties on 62 Squadron had been those of an armourer.

Dear Sir,

Being an ex-member of the RAF, and also of No 62 (B) Squadron, I thought it my duty to write and inform you of other acts of bravery carried out by Officers and N.C.O.s of 62 Squadron, besides the recent one published in the papers about Squadron Leader Arthur Scarf, for which he was awarded the V.C. (Posthumous). During the Far East campaign, our Squadron operated for a short time from Kulang airfield in the state of Johore (Malaya).

One day word was received that Japs were sailing down the west coast of Malaya in barges, in the Port Swettenham area.

Their plan being to land behind our troops fighting North of Port Swettenham, and cut them off.

Our Squadron was selected to carry out the operation of destroying the barges filled with Jap troops.

Only two aircraft were required as it was considered unsuitable to send the whole squadron as the enemy air opposition was so overwhelming.

We loaded the two aircraft to capacity with 40 and 20 lb 'Fragmentation' bombs, even stowing some on the flare rack in the wings.

In the meanwhile, F/O Haigh (ex-Wearn's Airways pilot), who joined the RAF in Singapore, and was posted to 62 Squadron had volunteered to Captain one aircraft, and F/Lt Lancaster the other.

F/O Haigh's crew consisted of F/Sgt Bowie, Bomb Aimer and Navigator, and F/Sgt Martin Rear Gunner.

F/Lt Lancaster's crew consisted of F/O Martin, Bomb Aimer and Navigator, and an Australian P/O, was the Rear Gunner, (I regret I cannot remember his name). The two old Blenheims struggled into the air, and headed for Port Swettenham, but they never returned.

During my evacuation by ship from Java, I met a Lance Corporal who served with the East Surrey Regiment in Malaya, and he said he was at Port Swettenham when the two Blenheims came over.

He informed me that just as our planes were about to attack the barges, about fifteen Jap 'Zero' fighters attacked them fiercely, setting them both on fire. Regardless of this, the pilots stuck to their course, and dived down and jettisoned their bombs on the barges killing hundreds of Jap troops.

Both planes crashed near the beach and exploded, the crews were believed to have perished.

The other act of bravery took place off the coast of Sumatra near Palembang. Our Squadron then being stationed at an air strip (code No. P2), about thirty miles from Palembang.

News was received that a large Jap invasion force was heading by sea for Palembang, all our aircraft were bombed up, and took off to attack the invaders. (We were re-equipped with Hudson aircraft just before we evacuated Singapore.)

One of our aircraft flown by F/O 'Cocky' Robinson, was severely damaged by 'Flak' from a Jap cruiser, and was practically uncontrollable.

His aircraft was too low for the crew to escape by parachute, so F/O Robinson forced his aircraft into a dive straight at the Jap Cruiser, striking it just behind the funnel.

There was a terrific explosion and I believe the cruiser sank two hours later.

F/O Robinson and crew (names not known) were presumed to have been killed instantly.

Flight Lieutenant Lancaster's home, was Colwyn Bay, N. Wales.

F/O Haigh's home was Singapore, but I think his parents lived at Hooton, Cheshire.

My reason for not informing you sooner of these facts is, I thought some of the Officers of our Squadron, who returned to the U.K. long before I did, would surely have informed you. Having read only recently of Squadron Leader Scarf's award, I presumed nothing had been mentioned to the Air Ministry of the other brave acts carried out by 62 Squadron.

If you require further proof of my statement, I am sure other ex-members of 62 Squadron, who served in the Far East, will verify this.

I remain Sir

Your obedient Servant,

(Sgt) T. Hayes.

The details from the Commonwealth War Graves Commission do not give any address details for Flying Officer Geoffrey William Haigh but it is generally agreed that he had Australian connections. The CWGC notes that he was 33 years old and married to Mary Agnes Haigh. Flight Lieutenant Norman Douglas Lancaster was indeed from north Wales and came from Deganwy. Both were subsequently Mentioned in Dispatches but it is not know whether this was due to the intervention of former Sergeant Hayes or the recommendation of Harley.

Flying Officer John Stewart 'Cocky' Robinson was 21 years old and came from Stewkley in Buckinghamshire. Unlike the other two he did not receive any recognition for his bravery. Whether or not Harley even replied to the Air Ministry, or if he did, what he wrote is not known. At this time he was quite ill and he may have been unable to respond and no reply was found with the letters amongst his personal papers

The fact that Harley's active service with the RAF had effectively ended, caused a lot of financial problems and worry for his wife Pat and, in May 1946, she left India for the last time and went to stay with her family in Perth. Pat and 3 year old Sallie later sailed to Durban and then spent two days travelling on a train to Johannesburg, where they set up home in part of the city called Booysens. Sallie thinks that her mother must have had a small RAF pension but they were very poor and the apartment was barely furnished, with just a bed and single chair. Sallie has said that she only saw her father twice in two years as families were not encouraged to visit the hospital because TB was seen almost as a social disease.

Back in England, three weeks after Harley had arrived in Pretoria, Group Captain Irving's recommendations were acted upon and on 21 June 1946, it was announced in a supplement to the *London Gazette* that Squadron Leader Arthur Scarf had been awarded the Victoria Cross. It was four-and-a-half years since Pongo had died of his wounds and although many of the records of RAF operations during that period have either been lost or destroyed, it proved that his outstanding bravery had not gone unnoticed.

Air Ministry 21 June 1946

The King had been graciously pleased to confer the posthumous award of the Victoria Cross to the under mentioned Officer in recognition of most conspicuous bravery.

Squadron Leader Arthur Stewart King Scarf (37963), Royal Air Force, No 62 Squadron.

In his youth Pongo had attended King's College School in Wimbledon that had a fine tradition dating back to 1829 when it had been founded as the junior department of King's College of London University. In 1908 it had been separated from the university and it had become an independent school in 1912. Like all those schools whose pupils received honours, it was keen to publicize the fact that one of its old boys had been awarded the highest accolade in the land. The day after the citation was published, on 22 June 1946, the *Daily*

Mail featured a story about Arthur, with the headline, 'The Head Tells The Story of Scarf V.C.'

Mr H.J. Dixon was the headmaster at King's College and he was a very proud man when he read the citation out to the boys, recalling the fact that Arthur had been, 'A pleasant boy, not frightfully bracing, but a fine ordinary chap'. He said that the young Arthur had played a steady un-sensational game of rugby but unfortunately he had never made the rugger fifteen. The headmaster also remembered that Arthur had been quite mad about aeroplanes!

The investiture took place on 30 July 1946 at Buckingham Palace and Sallie Gunn, Arthur's widow, announced to the press that she was going to attend and accept the Victoria Cross on behalf of her late husband. Exactly when the news of events at home filtered through to Harley in South Africa is not known, but he did know, because a copy of Group Captain Irving's recommendation was found amongst his personal papers.

Harley would have been very proud and humbled to hear of Pongo's award but he was probably still a little too weak to celebrate. He himself was later to receive six campaign medals including the Africa Star and the Pacific Star. His awards also included an Oak Leaf for being Mentioned in Dispatches but he never got the medals or recognition that many thought he deserved. That probably never bothered him personally but it was another disappointment to add to those of being refused a permanent commission and being medically discharged.

CHAPTER 6

Rhodesia and Retirement

Harley was transferred from Pretoria to Baragwanath Military Hospital, which was a TB sanatorium near Soweto on the outskirts of Johannesburg, where he spent the best part of two years. Although, as Sallie has pointed out, TB was seen as something of a social disease and visits were rare, there was a royal visit to the hospital on Saturday 5 April 1947. On that occasion Princess Margaret visited Baragwanath and was introduced to staff and patients and Harley's wife Pat and daughter Sallie were proud to be amongst the honoured guests.

Harley remained in hospital in South Africa for two years and he was finally discharged from the Royal Air Force on medical grounds in March 1948. The permanent commission that he had first applied for in 1939 had finally alluded him.

It is possible that Harley might have returned home but after being away for so long he may well have felt alienated from British culture and so he set up a new life with his family in Bulawayo in Southern Rhodesia. Harley had always been interested in cars and it seemed only natural that he should turn his hobby into a business.

Initially Harley worked for Sadler's Motor Supplies in Bulawayo but soon afterwards he moved to United Motors as a manager, where he was involved in the buying and selling of cars, as well as their maintenance. The cars were mainly British models like MGs and Morris Minors but occasionally he dealt in more luxurious types. Most weekends Harley was either involved in rallying or racing his MGTF on a track at Heany Barracks just outside Bulawayo and he won several silver cups. Harley's father disapproved of motor sport and he wrote several long letters telling him what a dreadful waste of money it was. Although Harley and his father had a lot of mutual respect for one another the criticism had little effect and some time later Harley was elected president of Bulawayo Motor Club.

On 22 November 1951 there was an addition to the family when Pat gave birth to another daughter named Eve. She was born in Lady Rodwell Maternity Hospital in Bulawayo and the fact that Harley now had two young daughters meant that he had to work harder to provide for them. Having a wife who came from Australia and with both of his daughters being born outside the United Kingdom meant that Harley's family was a truly international one and he no longer had the traditional roots. He maintained regular contact with his father and his brother Duncan but there was never any suggestion that he should return to Britain.

One thing that Harley did want to do was to get back to flying or at least become involved with aviation in some capacity and, in 1962, he joined the Rhodesian Air Force Reserve. Even with his vast amount of flying experience, because of his age and ill health he could not genuinely hope to be allowed to command an aircraft, but he was able to use his organizational skills and knowledge to good effect. Although he held the RAF rank of honorary group captain, he was happy to loose the 'scrambled egg' on his hat and serve as a flight lieutenant in a logistical support role.

The Rhodesian Air Force had a number of strong connections with Britain and during the war, 44 Squadron (Rhodesia) was predominantly a unit manned by Rhodesians. In December 1941 it made history when it became the first unit to be equipped with the Avro Lancaster. A number of Rhodesian Air Force Squadrons also joined Fighter Command, the future Prime Minister, Ian Smith, being one such pilot who served in various European theatres.

Like Harley, Ian Smith had had a tough war and on 4 October 1943 he had been badly injured when he crashed while flying a Hurricane at Pembrey in Wales. He had broken his jaw, his arm and his shoulder and, although he underwent several operations involving plastic surgery on his face, half of it remained paralysed. Despite the fact that he was still in pain, Smith returned to operational flying and in 1944 he was shot down over the Po Valley in Italy and forced to bale out of his stricken aircraft. He teamed up with another three downed pilots, joined a band of Italian partisans and French resistance fighters and managed get back to the Allied lines. Harley obviously enjoyed the company of men like Ian Smith because they had similar backgrounds to himself and they could share their experiences.

When Rhodesia formed a federation with Nyasaland in 1953, the Rhodesian Air Force had expanded and received its first modern equipment in the form of the de Havilland Vampire. On 15 October 1954 the Rhodesian Air Force was officially renamed the Royal Rhodesian Air Force. The year that Harley joined,1962, it received twelve Hawker Hunter FAW9 (1 Squadron) ground attack aircraft to join the sixteen English Electric Canberra bombers (5 and 6 Squadrons) but the break up of the federation at the end of 1963 weakened its strength.

On 4 April 1964 Winston Field resigned as Prime Minister and Ian Smith took over from him to lead Rhodesia into a campaign for independence from Britain. What happened soon after that is well known and, on 11 November 1966, Ian Smith announced a Unilateral Declaration of Independence from Britain; it was a decision of far reaching consequences.

As well as his service with the Rhodesian Air Force Harley continued to be in regular employment but he later left United Motors and went to work as manager for Sager Motors. The company dealt mainly with Jaguar and Sallie says that they always had the latest model parked on their driveway. However she disliked the fact that, particularly with the E Type, her father tried to drive fast like Stirling Moss and although outwardly the car appeared to be glamorous it often made her feel sick.

The British embargo and blockade of trade with Rhodesia meant that Jaguar parts and cars were hard to come by and so Harley became the director of an assembly plant set up by Peugeot. The French broke the embargo and managed to get parts into Rhodesia via the port of Beira in Mozambique and Peugeot became the most popular model in the country. They were not luxury cars but functional and easy to maintain and so were popular with farmers and the plant built about twenty-five cars a day.

In the same year that UDI was announced, the RAF made a decision that each of its fleet of new Vickers VC10 transport aircraft should be named after airmen who had been awarded the Victoria Cross. The first VC10 was handed over to the RAF at Wisley on 7 July 1966 and it entered service with 10 Squadron that was based at Brize Norton in Oxfordshire. VC10, serial number XV109 was named *Arthur Scarf VC*. It was the last production VC10 Mk. C1 and it entered service with the RAF in July 1968.

The name of Squadron Leader Scarf was thus linked with legends from the First World War, like Edward Mannock (XV103), James McCudden (XV104) and Albert Ball (XV105). They were all Pongo's heroes from his schooldays and that his name should be ranked alongside theirs would have made him a very proud man. It was a wonderful tribute, not only to Pongo Scarf, but to Harley and all those airmen and officers that had served alongside him on 62 Squadron.

Probably having been influenced by her mother with stories about what had happened during the war, Harley's daughter Sallie decided to train as a nurse and, in 1968, she became a pupil midwife at Queen Victoria Maternity Hospital in Johannesburg. It was there in November that year that she met Alex, a medical student who, she claimed, undermined her by trying to take over all the mothers and deliveries that were under her charge. However the disagreement brought them closer together and in February 1969 they got engaged. Alex and Sallie were married in July 1969 but Alex did not complete his training until December, by which time he was working at Baragwanath Hospital in Soweto that then accommodated 200 patients; the same former military hospital and sanatorium where Harley had spent two years being treated for TB. Their first child, Jonathan, was born in August 1970 at the Queen Victoria Hospital in Johannesburg and their daughter Elaine was born exactly a year later. By 1972 Alex was working as a doctor in general practice when he and Sallie moved from Johannesburg to Kimberly.

A sad event occurred the following year when, after being married for thirty-one years, Harley and Pat were divorced. Both had been under a great deal of pressure and recent events as well as those in the past had conspired to break up their marriage. As he had done during the Second World War, Harley was engaged on active service with the Rhodesian Air Force and was spending a lot of time away from home.

From 1972 until 1980 when Robert Mugabe gained power, Rhodesia was involved in an internal conflict that was often ignored by the outside world. During what was known as the 'Bush War' and in his capacity as a reserve air force officer, Harley was actively involved in operations that were trying to stop white farmers being murdered by black freedom fighters. Apart from the horrific murders, farms were often plundered before being set on fire and the animals slaughtered.

Harley's main role was organizing supplies and setting up forward airfields, such as those at Kariba, Centenary, Mount Darwin and Chiping. A wide variety of aircraft operated from these airfields including Allouhette III and Lynx helicopters for observation duties. Vintage Dakotas were used to transport troops and equipment into the bush and they were used for battlefield support and 'Casevac' duties.

In June 1974 Alex and Sallie emigrated to Canada, a move that was made because of increasing social and political pressures in South Africa. Canada also offered many more opportunities and a brighter and securer future for their children. Their third child, another boy who they named Lee, was born in April 1975 at the Queen Victoria Hospital, London, Ontario.

After her divorce Pat Boxall remained in Rhodesia and she not only kept in regular contact with her daughter in Canada but also her old friend, Sallie Gunn who, by that time, had returned to live in England. After they had split up, Harley continued to live in Harare where he was a member of the Legion and the RAF Association and a prominent member on both committees. At one point he was the chairman of the Legion and the vice-chairman of the RAF Association and he was very much involved with welfare issues.

In November 1978 Harley was awarded the Rhodesian Air Force Military Forces Commendation (Non Operational). He was informed about the award in a letter written by the head of the Rhodesian Air

Force, Air Marshal F.W. Mussell OLM who, over the years, had commanded Nos. 1 and 2 Squadrons and the Thornhills forward air base, on 1 November.

Dear Harley,

I have pleasure in advising you that the Acting President has been pleased to approve the award to you of the Military Forces Commendation (Non-Operational).

I congratulate you on this award, which has been made in recognition of the work carried out by you during your long service in the Volunteer Reserve of the Rhodesian Air Force. Your citation records that this service has been characterized by consistent loyalty and devotion to duty.

Your award will be promulgated in the Government gazette and published in the local newspaper shortly.

Yours sincerely,
Frank Mussell.

The citation dated 11 November 1978 read:

Flight Lieutenant Boxall has the distinction of being the oldest and longest serving member of the Volunteer Reserve of the Rhodesian Air Force. He has made a significant contribution to the force, both on and off duty. In latter years he has served as an Administrative Officer in the field, a role in which his performance had always been highly commendable. His loyalty and devotion to duty throughout his 17 years of service has been an example to all his colleagues.

The Military Forces Commendation was a silver pick awarded to denote an act of bravery, distinguished service or continuous devotion to duty in the operational or non operational sphere. The medal that came with it was the General Service Medal and it was normally awarded for service on operations for the purpose of combating terrorist incursions. This had a ribbon with a red and blue stripe, with the lighter blue stripe in the middle displaying a thinner yellow stripe.

By the time that Harley left the Reserve in 1980, the Royal Rhodesian Air Force comprised eight squadrons, two ground training schools, a parachute training school and a photographic section. It was a modern well equipped force that was run on similar lines to the Royal Air Force which was not surprising, because many of its officers like Harley had previously served in the RAF. Despite the break from Britain, its traditions and high standards were maintained.

In later years Harley's thoughts were never very far away from the past and especially his time with 62 Squadron in Singapore and Malaya. On 20 November 1985 he wrote to the Commanding Officer of the Argyle and Sutherland Highlanders informing him about the time in December 1941 when he been given command of an AFV.

Sir,

I wonder if the following episode has found a place in the annals of your illustrious regiment.

An armoured car (AFV) manned by the aircrew of the Royal Air Force covered part of the strategic withdrawal of the Argyle and Sutherland Highlanders down the GRIK ROAD – the arterial road, some 200 miles long, connecting KOTA BHARU on the north-east coast of Malaya with the main north-south road through IPOH and thence to SINGAPORE. KOTA BHARU had already fallen to the Japanese.

The remainder of the letter dealt with events on the Grik Road that have already been covered in Chapter One (Part 2) but it was a credit to the Royal Mail and the Post Office that it ever reached its destination because it was only addressed to the 'The Commanding Officer Scotland' of the Argyle and Sutherland Highlanders. Rather remarkably, Harley did get a reply from Lieutenant Colonel Neilson but he had to wait for seven months.

Lieutenant Colonel G.A. Neilson

Commanding 1st Battalion The Argyle And Sutherland Highlanders

5 June 1986

Dear Group Captain,

Thank you so much for your letter dated 20 November

1985. It has taken all this time to catch up with us, probably due to two unit moves in the last five years.

I read you letter with interest, everything must have seemed total confusion to all the young men caught up in the battles, delaying actions and retreats which are now part of history. Your enquiry deals with the exploits of our 2nd battalion, the famous 93rd, who were involved in a series of actions right down the peninsula.

As you probably already know, the delaying actions and especially the one at the Grik Road, were helping to gain time to prepare the defences further south. The 93rd was badly mauled at the Battle of Slim River where, with inadequate defensive weapons, the Japanese overwhelmed them and eventually only 3 officers and 90 other ranks reached Singapore.

Your letter will be passed to our regimental Headquarters where it will be disseminated to the appropriate Malayan campaign veterans who survived the disastrous Fall of Singapore in February 1942.

I hope that life in Zimbabwe is a lot easier. Our best wishes for the future and thanks again for writing.

Reading the reply Harley might have pondered about how lucky he had been to escape from the clutches of the Japanese at Alor Star, Taiping and on the Grik Road. Not only had 62 Squadron lost all its aircraft but the Argyle and Sutherland Highlanders had lost the best part of a battalion. How many of those eventually escaped from Singapore is not known.

A copy of Harley's letter was sent to Brigadier Ian Stewart who had commanded the 2nd Battalion, Argyle and Sutherland Highlanders in 1941 and also to Brigadier David Wilson who had commanded the armoured section. Lieutenant Colonel Wood also wrote to Harley and informed him that, in 1982, the Regiment had commissioned a painting of the crossing of the causeway from Malaya to Singapore and an armoured car was featured in it. Harley was informed that if he ever visited Scotland he had an open invitation to look them up and see the painting for himself.

Sallie Gunn died in 1986 of a respiratory infection aged 70. Over the years Harley's former wife Pat had kept touch with Sallie, but as the years went on their correspondence became less frequent. The final letter that Sallie wrote to Pat is dated 26 February 1986 and at that time she was living in Rotherfield, East Sussex. For Sallie, the past was also never very far away and she admitted in her letter:

> I still had nightmares after I was married to Stuart – and one night I cried my heart out as I suddenly remembered the two infant TB spines that we had in Alor Star which I had completely forgotten in all the turmoil! – Oh I wonder what happened to the dear helpless mites – I remember asking Pongo if we could adopt them when the war was over! But there were so many tragedies – remember meeting many nationalities on my way down from A. Star, on their way to blow bridges etc. Told them Japs were on our heels but nobody took any notice. They just obeyed orders.

Pat Boxall died on 26 September 1990 while on trip to Canada to stay with her daughter Sallie and her body was cremated locally. Events over the years had taken their toll on her and all the family, and Sallie and her sister Eve felt very bad about what had happened. Pat was 83 years old and she had survived so much in her life; the evacuation of Singapore where so many nurses were murdered and long sea voyages to Australia and South Africa. Pat had seen Harley through more than two years of ill health and she had been badly affected by the break up of their marriage.

Pat's old friend, Baiji Singh, was last heard of living in the State Palace in Jodphur, which to make ends meet, was converted during the 1970s and named the Umaid Bhawan Palace Hotel. It is just less than two miles from a new airport that opened in 1978. Baiji eventually succumbed to the charms of a man whom she married and had three children. The hotel, which has thirty-two air-conditioned rooms is a flourishing business. Jodhpur is one of the most popular tourist destinations in India and it now markets itself as 'Sun City'.

In June 1988 Harley visited Britain for the first time since 1944. He had a lot to catch up on and one of the places that he visited was the RAF Museum at Hendon. He also met up with old friends such as Wing Commander Frank Griffiths with whom he had served on 62 Squadron. By 1943 Frank had returned to England and was posted to Bomber Command to fly the Halifax. On 14 August that year his aircraft was shot down but he evaded capture and he later wrote a book about his experiences called *Angels*.

Sallie has suggested that by 1988 her father was missing England and he might have been looking to return and settle down. However he still had his roots and many friends in Zimbabwe and although the 'Old Country' might have been calling, he decided to return home. Maybe it was the sudden realization that he might never have the opportunity to visit Britain again that caused him to question where he was to spend his final years. In any case it must have been a difficult and emotional time for him on the journey back to Zimbabwe where the political situation was changing for the worse.

On 31 December 1988 Harley retired, after working for Peugeot for over twenty-two years, and in that time he had helped to produces a total of 27,000 cars. Rather ironically Robert Mugabe's freedom fighters also liked the Peugeot cars because of their ruggedness and after the Bush War ended Harley sold a good number to his supporters. The death knell came when Robert Mugabe nationalized the assembly plant and although as a director, Harley could have chosen to continue working, he was bitterly disappointed at the course of events and his health began to deteriorate as a result. First of all he was diagnosed with chronic leukaemia but that condition was later changed to acute leukaemia.

After being seriously ill for six months, Harley died at his home in Borrowdale, Harare, on 24 November 1994, with his new wife Gladys by his bedside. Harley's body was cremated at Warren Hills Crematorium and his ashes scattered at Borrowdale Anglican Church, where a brass plaque was mounted in his memory. It reads simply, 'Fly High Valiant Hero,' and arranging for it be made and put in place was one of the last things that his daughter Sallie did, before flying back to Canada. Harley was 81 years old and the causes of his death on his death certificate, were 1. Myeloid Leukaemia. 2. Cerebral Thrombosis.

As one can imagine, Sallie loved her father very much and was deeply saddened by his death, as was her sister Eve, who had by now moved to Perth, Western Australia, where their mother had grown up. Sallie remembers her father for many things but particularly for being meticulous in everything that he did. His clothes were always colour sorted, matched and neatly folded in his wardrobe and she recalled that his filing system was immaculate too. It is for that reason that so many of his documents and personal papers survived, as well as the fact that Harley's widow, Gladys, thought it best that Sallie should have them. Most of all, Harley was a very determined man and of the many things that Sallie learned from him, the most valuable one was never to take 'No' for an answer.

Apart from Sallie, Harley's only other immediate family was his brother Duncan who had returned to England after the war, married and settled down in the West Country. Duncan had suffered his own share of tragedy and, in September 1962, his wife Peggy, who was only in her mid-forties, died while undergoing an operation. They had four children and he later married Ann and has happily survived to be 93 years old.

Harley had lived through Britain's most difficult times and one of the most turbulent periods in the history of the Royal Air Force and there were many tributes to him, including an obituary that appeared in the Rhodesian Legion Magazine, *The Bell*. He had served in the RAF for twelve years but in the Rhodesian Air Force Reserve for seventeen, and it was fitting that one of his colleagues from that force should give the finest tribute of Harley's work with the Legion and Royal Air Forces Association. The letter from Wing Commander Roy Nichols was sent to Harley's widow, Gladys.

Dear Gladys,

Having only returned to Zimbabwe on the 6 December, I was astounded to learn from Jannell yesterday, of Harley's passing.

Words can not express my feelings at the sad news; apart from being an active member of the Committee, and my Vice Chairman, he was also a quiet, but dignified contributor to our decision making at the meetings.

On the many occasions that I have been out of the country,

Harley 'stood in' in for me admirably, even at the National Conference, and I am very grateful for, and appreciative of, the effort that he expended on both his Legion and RAFA involvements.

He will be sorely missed by us all in The Legion, but even more so by the Committee and myself since his untimely passing has robbed me of a total of three staunch supporters this year!! Steve Comberbach some weeks ago: John Salt some months ago, and now Harley…Not a good year!!

I have contacted 'Bob' Reynolds in Banket and passed on the news, since he and Harley were deeply involved in V.R. affairs during our last altercation, and frequently enquired after him (and his Jaguar).

If there is ANY consolation in his passing, it must be the speed with which it happened, since I believe, like most of us now, that the thought of a long and protracted – often painful – decline, leaves one with little or no dignity at the end. I know that the shock to yourself must be immense at this time, but believe me that you will, in time, come to terms with your great loss, of a husband, officer and gentleman.

You know that, should there be any way in which The Legion can assist you, you only have to ask.

Yours in sorrow.

C.R. Nichols. Wing Commander. D.M.M.

Chairman.

Former Premier Ian Smith also sent his condolences and, having been the chairman of the Royal Air Forces Association in Harare, he knew Harley quite well. He had just suffered his own loss as his wife Janet, whom he had married in 1948, had died just a few days before Harley.

For Sallie, living in Canada, there is no grave to put flowers on, or a living memorial like the VC10, XV109, that carries the name of Arthur Scarf but she sees those things that are associated with him, as being directly connected with memories of her father. They were good friends for over three years and they shared many experiences, such as joining 62 Squadron, converting to the Blenheim and flying

9,000 miles to Singapore. For another year-and-a-half after they both married in 1941, their close friendship extended to their wives and much of their off-duty time was spent in each others' company. They had flown the first sortie together after the Japanese invaded and they had shared the risks on the day that Pongo was killed.

On Monday 25 September 2006 Sallie and her husband Alex were invited to visit Brize Norton and they were shown around the VC10, XV109, *Arthur Scarf VC*. For most of its life the aircraft served with 10 Squadron but when it disbanded on 14 October 2005, the VC10 was handed over to 101 Squadron. In its original role it was a transport aircraft capable of carrying 137 passengers but with 101 Squadron it became part of the airborne tanker fleet involved in air-to-air-refuelling. At the time of writing in July 2009, XV109 is still in service and is expected to remain operational for at least another two years when the VC10 fleet will be phased out.

During their visit, Sallie and Alex were taken on board XV109 by Squadron Leader David Currie who allowed them to sit in the cockpit, where Sallie told him the story of Arthur Scarf and why he had been awarded the Victoria Cross. She also talked about her mother's connections and long-standing friendship with his widow, Sallie Gunn. They were treated as honoured guests of 101 Squadron and felt privileged to be given a tour of the station and the hospitality of the Officers' Mess.

The following day they visited the RAF Museum at Hendon and were shown around by the curator of medals and heraldry, Andrew Cormack. Sallie was allowed to see and hold Squadron Leader Scarf's Victoria Cross and it was the first time that anyone, other than museum staff, had touched it for many years. After Sallie Gunn had accepted the medal in 1946, she decided to it would be more appropriate if it remained with his immediate family and she gave it to Arthur Scarf's 10 year old nephew, John. However Arthur Scarf's sister thought that he was too young to be responsible for such an important piece of family history and so they gave it, on loan, to the RAF Museum, where it remains to this day.

In August 1939 when the Blenheims of 62 Squadron lifted off the runway at Cranfield and began their long journey to the Far East it was the beginning of a new era that changed the lives of many who made the journey. A large number of officers and airmen would never return and are buried in far-flung corners of Britain's former Empire. Altogether 62 Squadron lost 246 officers and airmen and seventy-five of those are mentioned on the Singapore Memorial, the majority of them having been either killed or taken prisoner in the wake of the Japanese attack on Malaya in late 1941. They have no known graves and the fate of many of them has never been determined.

After the war the body of Squadron Leader Arthur Scarf VC was exhumed from the makeshift grave near the hospital at Alor Star and he was one of seven former 62 Squadron personnel to be re-buried in Taiping War Cemetery in Malaysia. His grave, 2.G. 14, is visited regularly by officers of the Royal Malaysian Air Force and they have the utmost respect for him and all those RAF airmen who died while defending their country in 1941. His grave is also occasionally visited by officials from the United Kingdom and in December 2008 Colonel Paul Edwards MBE paid his respects. It was one of his last duties as Defence Attaché in Malaysia and he laid a wreath and sent back a number of photographs to mark the occasion.

Harley's ashes were scattered at Borrowdale Anglican Church and, like his old friend Pongo, with the exception of his brief visits to England in 1944 and 1948, he was destined never to return to his native land. Thus the two men had different fates, but effectively the same outcome, by the fact that they were both buried '...in a corner of a foreign field', the only difference being that Harley's final resting place was determined by choice.

The word 'devotion' appears regularly both in Harley's memoirs and in a number of letters and documents that either referred to him or were written about him. It does appear that to use Harley's own words, he was genuinely 'devoted to a calling' and that calling was not only to serve his country and help others, but to record a unique period of history that led up to the end of the British Empire. Had Harley not kept and filed the many photographs, letters and personal documents, then this detailed account of RAF life in the mid-1930s and events during the war in Malaya and India would have been forgotten.

Bibliography

Bowyer, Chaz, *For Valour: The Air VCs*, Caxton Editions, 2002

Fielding Stan, *Life in the Blue with 62*, self published, 2000

Probert, Air Commodore Henry, *The Forgotten Air Force: The Royal Air Force in the War Against Japan 1941-45*, Brassey's, 1996

Smith, Colin, *Singapore is Burning: Heroism and Surrender in World War 2*, Viking, 2005

Warner, Colin, *The Bristol Blenheim: A Complete History*, Crecy Publishing 2005

Wynn, Humphrey, *Forged in War: A History of RAF Transport Command 1943-1967*, TSO, 1996

Index